D1528773

Authority and
Female Authorship
in Colonial America

KEEP WITHIN COMPASS AND YOU SHALL BE SURE, TO AVOID MANY TROUBLES WHICH OTHERS ENDURE. KEEP WITHIN COMPASS

KEEP WITHIN COMPASS

A Virtuous Woman is a Crown to her Husband.

ENTER NOT INTO THE WAY OF THE WICKED, AND GO NOT IN THE PATH OF EVIL MEN.

Authority and Female Authorship in Colonial America

WILLIAM J. SCHEICK

THE UNIVERSITY PRESS OF KENTUCKY

Publication of this volume was made possible in part by a grant
from the National Endowment for the Humanities.

Editorial and Sales Offices: The University Press of Kentucky
663 South Limestone Street, Lexington, Kentucky 40508–4008

02 01 00 99 98   1 2 3 4 5

Frontispiece: Keep Within Compass, a late 18th-century illustration
admonishing young women about the perils of impropriety. Artist unknown

Library of Congress Cataloging-in-Publication Data
Scheick, William J.
  Authority and female authorship in colonial America / William J.
Scheick.
    p. cm.
  Includes bibliographical references (p.   ) and index.
  ISBN 0-8131-2054-3 (alk. paper)
  1. American literature—Colonial period, ca. 1600-1775—History
and criticism. 2. Women and literature—United States—History—
18th century. 3. Women and literature—United States—History—
17th century. 4. American literature—Women authors—History and
criticism. 5. Authority in literature. 6. Authorship.
I. Title.
PS186.S34 1998
810.9'9287'09032—dc21   97-28918

For
CATHERINE

Contents

Acknowledgments ix

Introduction 1

1. Authority and Witchery 27
Cotton Mather's Manual for Women
Mary English's Acrostic

2. Love and Anger 51
Anne Bradstreet's Verse Letter to Her Husband
Esther Edwards Burr's Letter-Journal

3. Captivity and Liberation 82
Elizabeth Hanson's Captivity Narrative
Elizabeth Ashbridge's Autobiography

4. Subjection and Prophecy 107
Phillis Wheatley's Poetry

Conclusion 128

Works Cited 133

Index 146

Acknowledgments

I have benefited from opportunities to present portions of this study at meetings of the American Literature Association (1992), the American Literature Association Symposium on Women Authors (1993), the South Central Modern Language Association (1993, 1996), the Associated Colleges of the South Women's Studies Conference (1995), and the Women's Studies Faculty Colloquium (1996). I am grateful to Charles Adams (University of Arkansas), Rosemary Fithian Guruswamy (Radford University), Sharon M. Harris (University of Nebraska), Nancy B. Johnson (University of New Orleans), Carla Mulford (Pennsylvania State University), Lou Ann Norman (University of Central Arkansas), and Lisa Moore (University of Texas at Austin) for these occasions. I also thank Dorothy Baker (University of Houston) for an observation made at one of these meetings and both Leah Marcus (University of Texas at Austin) and Bernard Rosenthal (State University of New York at Binghamton) for their support of this book during its composition. A grant awarded through the agency of the University Research Institute of the University of Texas at Austin, overseen by former president Robert M. Berdahl and former vice president William S. Livingston, enabled me to complete this work while on leave from the classroom.

Parts of this book were also published in earlier versions: "Phillis Wheatley's Appropriation of Isaiah," *Early American Literature* 27 (1992): 135–40; "Logonomic Conflict in Bradstreet's 'Letter to Her Husband,'" *Essays in Literature* 21 (1994): 166–84; "Friendship and Idolatry in Esther Edwards Burr's Letters," *University of Mississippi Studies in English* n.s. 11–12 (1993–95): 138–50; "Authority and

Witchery: Cotton Mather's *Ornaments* and Mary English's Acrostic," *Arizona Quarterly* 51 (1995): 1–32; "Subjection and Prophecy in Phillis Wheatley's Verse Paraphrases of Scripture," *College Literature* 22 (1995): 122–30; and "Logonomic Conflict in Hanson's Captivity Narrative and Ashbridge's Autobiography," *The Eighteenth Century: Theory and Interpretation* 37 (1996): 3–21. The publication of these earlier explorations provided encouragement for this larger undertaking, and so I acknowledge my indebtedness to editors Bruce Clarke, Edgar A. Dryden, Benjamin Franklin Fisher, Philip Gura, Thomas Joswick, and Jerry McGuire. Having served as editor of *Texas Studies in Literature and Language* from 1975 to 1992, I know something of the nature of their enterprise.

It is time, too, at this late point in my professional life to express a retrospective thanks to all those—and they have been many—who for more than thirty years have countenanced my critical endeavors. Their generosity has given me the career that I know and enjoy today, a very special gift I can never fully reciprocate. Everything considered, I know that professionally I have indeed been very fortunate.

I have especially been fortunate in the friendship of Catherine Rainwater (St. Edward's University), who over the years has often unselfishly diverted attention from her own scholarly pursuits in order to attend to my undertakings. *Amicus est tanquam alter idem.*

Introduction

Among the many revisions that have occurred in studies of colonial America, three in particular influence my investigation in this book. There was, we now recognize, much more trouble with the establishment of authority in the New World settlements than we had once thought. Relatedly, we understand better today that Puritan culture, early and late, was far more diverse and heterodoxic—far less formed—than we had previously believed. And we now appreciate better that within both of these dynamic contexts, women's voices were more evident and distinctive than we had once noticed. These voices, wittingly or unwittingly, dialogued over the franchise of authority and, as a result, often revealed other stories within the main story of a still unfolding theocratic orthodoxy, including the Puritan version.

One story told by these women concerns the discomfort some of them experienced when expressing a sense of identity, a discomfort that registered beneath the surface of their writings and sometimes unstabilized their efforts as writers. This problem can be gauged not only by effects in their own work. Clues to their difficulties also surface as "another story" in writings by male authors (Cotton Mather, for example) who, in one way or another, touch upon the subject of female authority. My book tries to piece together a version of this "other story."

This is the story I did not recount in my *Design in Puritan American Literature* (1992), which explored a narrative phenomenon identified as the logogic site. A logogic site is a textual locus where the author or reader is invited to hesitate and contemplate the confluence of secular and divine meanings. This convergence of historical connotation and eternal denotation in Puritan writings is authorized by the Logos's Christic incarnation, which in Augustinian tradition reaffirms the union of matter and spirit in creation. Literary play at these textual points, however, evidences various degrees of authorial anxiety. In Puritan literature the complex interweaving of the artist's craft and the Creator's artistry at these sites of dual signification provided one means of negotiating authorial pride in potentially idolatrous personal expression, on the one side, and authorial humility in possibly revealing God's concealed aesthetic design, on the other side. Through close attention to logogic cruxes, I suggested, we can better appreciate a noteworthy property of Puritan aesthetics.

Authority and Female Authorship in Colonial America is a companion to this earlier volume, a companion with a different story to tell about a related narrative feature. The focus of this book is on sites of logonomic conflict. *Logonomic conflict* refers to peculiar, sometimes subversive, narrative effects that demarcate certain tensions extant within culturally regulated ideological complexes. *Ideological complexes* are "contradictory versions of the world, either coercively imposed by one social group on another on behalf of its own distinctive interests or subversively offered by another social group in attempts at resistance in its own interests." These ideological complexes operate within *logonomic systems,* which are visible "rules [*nomos*] prescribing the conditions for [the] production and reception of meanings [*logos*]" (Hodge and Kress 1988, 3-5). Logonomic systems express deeply entrenched efforts by dominant groups to control, and to legitimate their control over, subordinated groups through the reciprocal media of ideas and language (Hodge 1990, 12). But the cultural discourses whereby these systems contain opposition or exceptions to general rules inadvertently acknowledge the friction and contradictions at the core of all ideological complexes. Sites of logonomic conflict, as my study shows, provide various narrative signs of the ideological contradiction and friction typical of cultural systems.

As applied in this book, logonomic conflict inverts the logogic crux, as defined in my previous examination. Whereas in that study logogic cruxes are identified as textual moments when the quotidian and the divine are anxiously commingled, sites of logonomic conflict can be glimpsed in the unintentional, barely perceptible ruptures occasioned by an author's uneasy attempt to negotiate between orthodox and personal authority. These sites, in contrast to logogic cruxes, neither necessarily feature religious concerns nor usually register moments of deliberate authorial contemplation. Most often, writers and their contemporaries seem unaware of any ideological dissonance within the textual management of the visible prescriptive rules of their cultural logonomic systems. Nevertheless, *unconscious* resistant impulses lurk beneath the surface of their various narrative strategies, strategies authorized by the prevailing systems of their cultural milieu. The seismic activity of these impulses is underground, with only subtle, hardly detectable disruptive effects on the surface of a work. For the most part, in contrast to the logogic crux, these loci of disruption, of logonomic conflict, mar aesthetic design. For the *most* part—for when writers such as Phillis Wheatley consciously exploit sites of logonomic conflict, a different aesthetic mode emerges, a subterranean divergent art of deliberate resistance and revision.

My understanding of the unconscious here is of a general kind. It posits a background of mental processes of which one tends to be unaware. To venture much more than this ordinary definition of the unconscious is unhelpful because, regardless of what theory one might adopt, at present there is no adequate conception of the nature of consciousness, indeed of the mind as a whole, to encourage confidence in any particular psychological system. Whatever the unconscious may be, if anything at all finally, we have commonly attributed to it certain broad features such as described by the seventeenth-century Puritan philosopher Ralph Cudworth:

There may be some vital energy without clear and express "consense" and "consciousness, animadversion, attention" or "self-perception" . . . . Our human souls themselves are not always conscious of whatever they have

in them. . . . That vital sympathy by which our soul is united and tied fast
. . . to the body, is a thing that we have no direct consciousness of, but
only in its effects. . . . There is also [a] more interior kind of plastic power
in the soul . . . whereby it is formative of its own cogitations, which [it]
itself is not always conscious of. . . . Our human actions are not governed
by . . . exact reason, art, and wisdom, nor carried on with . . . constancy,
evenness[,] and uniformity. [1845, 1:246-51]

Cudworth's Platonism aside, the phrases most pertinent to my study
include "vital energy," "no direct consciousness of," and "only in
its effects."

The issue of effects is certainly complicated, especially since it
may be possible that conscious intentions can be informed or determined by unconscious impulses. However, it is only insofar as
these effects stand out in some manner from personal intention or
from social convention that they provide signs to that force which
we commonly designate as the unconscious. And conflict is a chief
feature of such effects, a feature observed from at least the eighteenth century to the present. The presence of these effects in the
writings under consideration in this study is identified as logonomic
conflict.

Authority

Authority is the matrix of logonomic conflict. As Foucault and new-
historicist studies have indicated, humanity engages authority by
way of an unresolved dialogism between resistance to and replica-
tion of the status quo (Foucault 1977, 151). The perception of authority is always "a process of interpretive power," so that "the
sentiments of authority lie in the eye of the beholder," who experiences both "fear and regret" in trying to penetrate the "secret the
authority [figure] possesses" (Sennett 1980, 20, 154). Colonial
American men, accordingly, were not exempt from this struggle
despite the fact that they were more favorably aligned than were
women with the power structures of their time—that is, with the
logonomic systems of set "rules prescribing the conditions for [the]

production and reception of meanings." Thomas Paine, in a particularly theatrical example, achieved his own voice by means of a precarious and paradoxical opposition to established father figures, whose rhetorical strategies he appropriated in asserting his sense of personal identity (Davidson and Scheick 1994). My essayed configuration of the framework of women's responses to authority is, therefore, not designed to argue for exclusivity at every turn of its commentary; it is, instead, designed to recover something of the range of this colonial female response, even when such response necessarily overlapped with that of colonial males.

In both cases, however, hesitation is in order when speaking about the status of men and the status of women in social arrangements (Whyte 1978), especially in preindustrial communities such as those of colonial North America. In societal structures involving both genders, power relations tend to be so subtly dispersed that the exertion of authority by one gender in a specific communal sector does not necessarily translate into a similar role in every other sector. In colonial America, for instance, women experienced fairly distinct spheres of influence, such as the practice of healing witchcraft, a point we shall observe in the next chapter. Nor should we overlook the capacity of women to exert considerable informal influence beyond what they are officially granted by their societies. A totalization of the status of women is accordingly not intended in my discussion, even if the convenience of a kind of rhetorical shorthand may occasionally appear to suggest such an unsound approach.

With this caveat in mind, I venture as my point of departure a reasonable proposition, given what we currently know of colonial American culture: In the northeastern region during the seventeenth and eighteenth centuries female encounters with authority were on the whole qualitatively dissimilar to male encounters with authority. Emphasizing *on the whole* here is important because, as mentioned earlier, certain elements of women's equivocal attempts to conform to authorized patterns of behavior and thought were not notably distinctive from those of their male contemporaries. Nevertheless, although there doubtless were several significant similarities (and not only in the writings of dissident men such as John Wheelwright) between colonial male and female responses to prevailing cultural hegemonies, the difference in the nature of their gender alignment with an androcentric power structure suggests that male responses to authority could not have been precisely identical to those of their relatively disfranchised female partners. That the colonial legal definition of adultery, for example, emphasized fornication with a married woman and excluded sexual relations between married men and single women, and that the female victim of rape was expected to rely on her father or husband (as the custodian of her body) to determine the nature of her response are typical indications of gender differences in the area of social authority. My goal in the chapters that follow is to describe experiences, as represented in writings by colonial women, that convey features indicative of the panoply of female responses to authority, even if some of these responses were also sometimes expressed by men.

Since there were several communal contexts in which they were excluded from male modes of identity formation, it has been argued (Miller 1986, 111), women managed an alternative negotiation of the dominant social text. During the seventeenth and eighteenth centuries, in England as well as in its colonies, women appear to have struggled with authority more personally and more internally than did most of their male peers. As the word "more" suggests, the difference was a matter of degree, but it appears to have been a real difference nonetheless. For instance, although little is known about the province of reading and writing among early modern women in England, we do know that a number of them in aristocratic families struggled (usually in a masked manner) to authorize both resistance and self-definition through authorship (Lewalski 1993, 1-11, 313-14). A specific indication of such a struggle is observable in the marketplace strategy adopted by some eighteenth-century English women writers, including New York–born Charlotte Lennox in *The Female Quixote* (1752). Capitalizing on the uncertain signification of female identity, these authors suggested that their writings, as with women in general, were most like themselves when paradoxically they were related to nothing because when they were related to historical antecedents (something), they were dispossessed of signification (Gallagher 1994, 145-202).

It is pertinent, too, to observe how European women dodged the issue of authority in their seventeenth- and eighteenth-century translations of scientific works. In these uncommon productions, in a discipline distinctly resistant to the inclusion of early-modern women, female achievement in thinking and writing—the apt language of their translations—was virtually screened behind the ideas of the translated male authors. The actual voice of these women— the somewhat more evident expression of their attainment—was demurely recorded in prefaces and footnotes (Findlen 1995, 173), a subordinate position that modestly relegated the issue of the authority of the female translator to the margin of her reader's attention.

Even Queen Elizabeth I, whom such seventeenth-century authors as Anne Bradstreet would later construe as a model of resolute authority (Schweitzer 1988; Sweet 1988), represented herself in terms of customary domestic female subservience, a calculated admission of the vulnerabilities of her gender designed to enable her with unconventional and unstable power (Berry 1989; Frye 1993, 28-55). She never escaped from the pervasive cultural notion that biblically, theologically, ecclesiastically, socially, and familially, women were the second sex. In the secular provinces of Quaker society, as well, women were considered the weaker sex in spite of their equality in religious matters. To be second, it hardly needs to be observed, is to be less empowered in relation to the theocratic authority that has defined one as secondary.

According to the traditionally hegemonic and selective readings of Genesis, the mother of mankind was not only created from Adam's rib on second thought (as it were), but through a weakness of mind she ruined paradise and engendered mortality. Reinforced by patristic, monarchic, and social authority, the northeastern colonial ministry customarily enhanced this reading of Genesis by relying on the Pauline espistles as the chief guide to the second sex.

Although without clarification Saint Paul seems to insist upon gender-based hierarchies in Corinthians and appears to eradicate such differences in Galatians (Boyarin 1993), Puritans like Mather were inclined to relegate the former notion to the quotidian and the latter to the afterlife. Seventeenth-century Christian dogma, in general, reflected an abiding dualism, even in the unitary belief in the Word made flesh (Staten 1993), and this feature is evident in the Puritan endorsement of the conviction that "the head of the woman is the man" (1 Cor. 11:3). As Cotton Mather wrote in 1726-27—over a hundred years into the Puritan colonial project—"as now it is," women's "Subjection to Men" is divinely sanctioned (Smolinski 1995, 266). In the theocratic context of such "necessary and useful Restraints of [their] sex," as Benjamin Colman put it (Turell 1735, 69), women were relegated to second-class citizenry within the family (where they were expected to "submit . . . as is fit" to their husbands [Turell 1735, 117]), the church (where in some communities they were assigned nonstatus seats), and the state (where frequently they were assigned minimal civil representation and denied property rights). Moreover, in a co-optative move, their identity was appropriated to depict the ideal saint's spiritual abjection (Schweitzer 1991, 1-35), their traditional roles were reassigned to male protagonists in Puritan works (Thickstun 1988, 20-23), and their biological distinction was displaced by a masculine definition of the new birth of the soul (Luxon 1995, 15-22).

Admittedly, there may have been another side to this pattern of subjugation. Possibly women generally ignored the male strategies of confiscation in this cultural representation of them and, instead, often unquestioningly drew from it a sense of the significance of their place and role. Some women may have instinctively derived manipulative strategies from the Puritan feminine ideal (Koehler 1980, 181-86); others may have appreciated its authorization of their specifically feminine influence, particularly in the domestic realm, as exemplary Christians (Porterfield 1992, 80-95). That such empowerment may have figured in women's sense of themselves is possibly suggested by their renegotiation of the boundaries of male authority in England during the Commonwealth. At that time, a number of women, emphasizing their traditional identification with virtue, argued for a more active female involvement in society (Hobby 1988, 13-18).

Such a potential response should not be underestimated. Neither should its appeal to women and its success in negotiating all of their feelings be overestimated. A delicate balance in speech and action was required for a colonial woman to conform to the prevailing standard of female respectability. This standard was often enforced by female gossip (Brown 1996, 306-18), which was influenced by a cultural imputation of the female proneness to deficiency. That Jane Colman Turell (1708-35) indicated her personal "Ambition of raising the honor of her Sex" (Turell 1735, 78) suggests that for her as doubtless for many others, colonial women's sense of authorized selfhood apparently included a self-conscious awareness of some general dishonor attributed to their gender. Furthermore, as we briefly noted, a substantial body of current discourse suggests that authorized identities are never secure, either in representation or in reception, but are always problematically relational for both male and female.

Julia Kristeva speculates on the opposition of the pre-Oedipal drive to subjectivized identity, for example. She points to a semiotic energy beneath language that is capable of producing a "wandering" that in turn disfigures the order of customary signification within the linguistic structure (1980, 136). A related *discours décousu,* a "poetics of interruptibility" featuring an associative (nonlinear) and episodic (nonconclusive) disjunctiveness in narrative form, has been detected in several documents by colonial women writers (Harris, 1996, 28). My study, while not grounded in Kristeva's theory of the unconscious, is likewise concerned with a type of distorted "wandering" that apparently registers several signs of difficulty in colonial women's acceptance of their social identity.

In the specific instance of northeastern colonial American women, evidence suggests some discomfort and instability in living within their culturally assigned place. This evidence ranges in degree. There were major disruptions, such as Anne Hutchinson's dissent (Lang 1987, 41-46). There were medium quakes, as suggested in Anne Bradstreet's justification of her poetry: "I am obnoxious to each carping tongue, / Who sayes, my hand a needle better fits" (McElrath and Robb 1981, 7). There were small tremors of discontent, as indicated in Cotton Mather's chastisement of "the Female Sex [who] may think they have some Cause to complain of us [men], that we stint them in their Education, and abridge them of many Points wherein they might be serviceable" (Smolinski 1995, 266). And there were subterranean tremors occasioning tiny faultlike fractures in female art, such as the writings explored in this study.

In short, whatever accommodations colonial women may have made to the status quo of their authorized identity, it was also utterly *natural* for them, given their situation, to experience swells of resistance varying in extent. (Colonial men, favored by the gender constructions of their day, presumably evinced such conflict at somewhat different personal sites.) Although contrary to each other, accommodation and resistance mutually involved sincerity and emotion. The women presented in the following chapters, for instance, were devout in their "conventional" religious sentiment, which overall was not compromised by the androcentric disposition of their theological beliefs. Equally genuine, of course, are the occasional intimations of resistance to the status quo that reveal other features of female identity, features contingently repressed by theocratic authority.

Whether intended or unintended, whether emphatic or understated, such resistance registers the unstable coalescence of both an anxious desire for authorization based on the inner province of personal feelings and a fretful belief in authorization based on the outer province of theocratic definition. At such moments, as the following chapters suggest, there is an unsettled and unsettling contest between—in contrast to the logogic site's potentially redemptive confluence of—subjectivized, secularly unauthorized connotative readings of experience and objectified, divinely authorized denotative readings of that same experience. Indeed, Anne Hutchinson may have implied as much by suggesting that human comprehension of the divine word is necessarily limited and that the meanings of words are contextually determined, not absolute in the ways her male inquisitors were using them to impose order, control, and closure to their arguments (Tobin 1990).

Both the logogic crux and logonomic conflict suggest occasions when authors remain unsure of their undertaking. But whereas logogic sites celebrate the miraculous intersection of the quotidian and the eternal despite the author's uncertain personal relationship to this intersection, colonial American female expression of logonomic conflict evinces no similar hope in a paradise regained. With the possible (albeit qualified) exception of Phillis Wheatley's example, these latter loci suggest a paradise lost—an exiled state defined by a mutually constitutive opposition between the theocratic and the personal, by an unrelieved dialogic tug-of-war over authority that ruptures every attempt at resolution.

Authorship

The verbal medium of this logonomic conflict was the male controlled discourse of church and state. That is to say, when individuals expressed their inner impulses, they did so in terms at once personal and public. This meant, as we shall see, an extensive use of biblical allusion, a prominent rhetorical currency of the time. Male mentors determined the credit of this currency, a credit with a long patristic history, and women tried to work within this androcentric interpretative framework, which they learned from the pulpit, discussion groups, and books. It is not surprising, then, that the "cadences, rhythms, vocabulary, phrases, and substance of the English Bible," so "interwoven into the fabric" of the work of their transatlantic peers (Otten 1992, 4), are likewise features of the writings of northeastern colonial women. Their documents mutually evidence close encounters with Holy Writ. In Medford, Massachusetts, for instance, Jane Colman Turell "read the Bible out in Course, once in a Year, the Book of Psalms much oftener, besides many

Chapters and a Multitude of Verses which she kept turn'd down in a Bible, which she had been the Owner and Reader of more than twenty Years" (Turrell 1735, 116).

But until eighteenth-century Quakerism, as we shall see in the example of Elizabeth Ashbridge, colonial female authors simply had no authority whatsoever to venture into the male preserve of scriptural interpretation; and among the colonists generally, the persecuted Quakers were hardly deemed suitable figures of authority. In the sixteenth century, Queen Elizabeth had cleverly appropriated the status of the prophet Daniel in a passing allusion that suggested divine intervention in her ascendancy to the throne (Frye 1993, 36), but her reference was too fleeting for its more profound implications to have registered upon her hearers, at least consciously. At the end of the eighteenth century in England, the emergence of Quaker-inspired female Methodist preachers met with strong negative reactions; as a result, male Methodist leaders during the first decade of the nineteenth century forbade female evangelism. Methodism was not influential in North America until the start of the nineteenth century (Wigger 1994, 167-68). At that time in the new Republic, it is pertinent to note, Hannah Adams (the author of the first American dictionary of world religions) was assailed by orthodox clergy not only for her liberal theology but also, and especially, for assuming the right to interpret Scripture and to publish her views in the male genre of theological treatises (Vella 1993).

Christian biblical commentary tradition, in short, was a well-established preserve of male authority, and it often gave the impression of male solidarity. For while biblical commentaries varied denominationally on certain contentious theological and liturgical matters (such as the virginity of Mary and the nature of the Lord's Supper), they more frequently agreed on the extensive undisputed biblical episodes. Matthew Henry's Presbyterian commentaries, preferred by clergy and laity alike, were typical in this regard. Henry's commentaries were so highly regarded throughout the eighteenth century that they were prevalent in numerous households (Greenslade 1963, 3:493) and, as a result, were long-lasting in their influence (Frerichs 1988, 4). For this reason, Henry's popular commentaries influence my observations about sanctioned Puritan readings of Scripture.

The official interpretations of the Bible were primarily disseminated from the pulpit, which was likely the primary source of northeastern colonial women's knowledge about certain scriptural passages. Women also encountered exegeses of Holy Writ in their reading of sermonic discourses and in their participation in discussion groups. During the eighteenth century many may have had domestic access to commentary volumes, such as Henry's well-known series. When these women utilized scriptural allusions in their writings, they in general deliberately tried to reflect the authorized male commentary tradition. But sometimes their use of biblical allusions inadvertently recorded underground impulses that resisted and altered the orthodox surface of their writings. Occurrences of this phenomenon in colonial writings by women may be understood as a form of transculturation, which has been described as a process whereby a subordinate social group appropriates and revises cultural matter transmitted by a dominate social community (Pratt 1992, 6).

If the use of biblical allusions potentially occasioned a submerged anxiety in women because such scriptural citation was circumscribed by male authority, writing itself was often another source of uneasiness. We already heard Anne Bradstreet defend herself against the charge that her "hand a needle better fits, / A Poets Pen, all scorne, I should thus wrong" (McElrath and Robb 1981, 7). Whatever may or may not have been ironic (Eberwein 1981) or specifically local in her retort here, she was also responding to the prevalent view of writing as a male preserve: "For such despight they cast on female wits: / If what I doe prove well, it wo'nt advance, / They'l say its stolne, or else, it was by chance" (McElrath and Robb 1981, 7).

A century later in *Poems on Divers Subjects* (1757), which appears to pay homage to Bradstreet's verse, a member of old-light Eleazor Wheelock's parish in Lebanon, Connecticut, likewise had to defend herself against a similar charge, specifically that she "borrowed her Poetry from [Isaac] Watts and others" (Brewster 1758, 22). Martha Wadsworth Brewster (fl. 1710-57) was indeed fond of Watts's work, even at one point (in an elegy about him) fantasizing that she was his unworthy "Heir" (25). To confute her accusers, however, Brewster participated in a public demonstration when she "Translate[d II Chronicles 6:16-17] into Verse, in a few Minutes Extempore" (22). It was not incidental that she included in her book this verse paraphrase of Scripture as well as a note concerning its origin. Given the eccentric occasion of this poem, the line in it that reads "Ye Creatures all, in vast Amazement stand" (22) possibly evinces some trace of personal nuance aimed at those who had attempted to deprecate Brewster's competence as a poet.

Concern with female literary composition could, in fact, be much more severe than denunciations such as women can at best write only by plagiarism or by accident. John Winthrop pointed to Anne Yale Hopkins, wife of the governor of Hartford, as "a godly young woman, and of special parts," who suffered "the loss of her understanding and reason . . . by occasion of her giving herself wholly to reading and writing, and had written many books" ([1908] 1959, 2:225).

"Delight in Reading," Brewster instructed her daughter (Brewster 1758, 34; Watts 1977, 25-27). "You must go on by Reading and Study to improve the Powers which God has given you," Colman advised his daughter, who under his guidance read by the age of two, wrote by the age of nine, and (like Anne Bradstreet nearly a century earlier) enjoyed unrestricted access to an extensive family library (Turell 1735, 69). So excessive reading, not reading per se, was potentially a problem for women. Inordinate reading and study, Harvard divine John Adams cautioned in 1757, can be the means whereby "too learned Females lose their Sex" (Colman 1735, iv).

Writing, in contrast to reading, was much more distinctly perceived as a male activity. The gendering of writing as a masculine activity has a long tradition, as Sando Botticelli's *Madonna del Magnificat* (c. 1483) dramatically suggests (Schibanoff 1994). In this painting, presenting a rare fifteenth-century image of a woman writing, Mary anonymously inscribes her magnificat only through the male agency of the Christ child, whose hand rests on hers holding the pen and thereby authorizes what she writes. During the seventeenth century and especially the eighteenth century, there were many more women who could write than there were in the fifteenth century. Nevertheless, such encouragement as Benjamin Colman gave his daughter in 1725—"With the Advantages of my liberal Education at School & College, I have no reason to think but that your Genius in Writing would have excell'd mine" (Turell 1735, 69)—was extremely rare. Nearly thirty years later, it is pertinent to note here, a scene in Charlotte Lennox's *Female Quixote* appears to correlate a young woman's illicit affair with her male writing instructor and the idea of female authorship as a form of transgressive cross-dressing (Marshall 1993).

In fact, as late as Hannah Webster Foster's didactic, if finally conflicted, *The Boarding School* (1798), there were post-Revolutionary warnings about the possibility of public censure hazarded by women who publish (Eldred 1993, 37). Somewhat earlier, in 1789, Annis Boudinot Stockton (1736-1801) likewise recorded her personal sense of the "risk of being sneered at by those who criticise female productions, of all kinds" (Mulford 1995, 10), an observation all the more significant given the numerous poems Stockton had published in many of the most prestigious periodicals of her day. In a 1756 letter by one of Stockton's early correspondents, Esther Edwards Burr's expression of fear and secrecy suggests the degree to which female interest in writing as a cultural pursuit and as an indication of identity could be experienced as a generally taboo activity:

The good woman inquired after you very kindly and desired me the next time I wrote to you to send her kindest regards to you—she said the next time I wrote—she does not know our method of corresponding—I would have told her, for I know her friendly heart would be pleased with it, but I was affraid she would tell her MAN of it, and *he* knows so much better about matters than she that he would sertainly make some Ill-natured remarks or other, and so these Hes shall know nothing about our affairs untill they are grown as wise as you and I are. [Karlsen and Crumpacker 1984, 183]

Burr's conspiratorial sarcasm is clear in this instance, as is her on-going concern with at-large male disapproval, when three months later she again tells her correspondent: "She dont know that I am always writing and I dare not tell her for fear she will tell her MAN[,] and everybody hant such a Man as I have about those things" (200). After the death of her progressive-thinking husband (as we will see in chapter 2) an intense moment of logonomic conflict surfaces in Burr's letter to her repressive father, Jonathan Edwards, who doubt-less would have completely disapproved of his daughter's secret sense of self-validation through authorship: "To tell the truth I love my self two well to be indifferent whether I write or no" (89).

Literacy

The teaching of reading to children was a common maternal re-sponsibility in seventeenth-century England and New England, whereas the teaching of writing only to boys was a paternal duty (Monaghan 1989). This fact, more than any other, explains why archival research has turned up so few documents penned by women (Ulrich 1982, 5). Obviously, as Anne Bradstreet's example particu-larly reveals, even early in the seventeenth century some northeast-ern colonial women could write, and certainly by the middle of the next century many more could do so. How many remains very much in dispute as a result of the inadequacy of our present understand-ing of colonial literacy (Bailyn 1960, 84; Cremin 1970, 664–65). Less in dispute by far is the extent of illiteracy among African Ameri-can women (Ingersoll 1994, 777), even deep into the eighteenth century; literacy, especially the mastery of writing, among slaves would not have reinforced their masters' control. As a fully literate black female slave, therefore, Phillis Wheatley was indeed a colo-nial cultural phenomenon.

Concerning American women of English origin, we do know that urban residents substantially outnumbered their village peers in literacy throughout the colonial period and that women in general continued to be taught reading alone long after writing had become a primary part of male instruction (Lockridge 1974, 38-42). We know that during the Boston subscription campaigns against the consumption of imports during the 1770s, women's lists carried several hundred signatures (Breen 1993, 490). However, we also know that the increased level of female signatures by 1795 (nearly 45 percent) evidently did not actually reflect an equal gain in the mastery of writing. The main reasons for skepticism here include the fact that signature percentiles always exceed those for actual writing ability and that women, in particular, were able "to 'fake' a smooth signature when totally illiterate" (Lockridge 1974, 126-27). Resistance to hasty conclusions concerning writing skills based on female signatures emerges as well in the Newbury town records, which may or may not be typical of broader regional practices; in this town, the children assigned to the care of the selectman from 1743 to 1760 were all instructed in reading, whereas only the boys were expected to learn "to write a Ledgable hand & cypher as far as the Gouldin Rule" (Ulrich 1982, 44).

In the southern colonies, as in the northern colonies, women were substantially less literate than were men (Bruce 1910, 1:454). This surmise is supported, albeit hardly proven, by a few available statistics. Documents from Elizabeth City County (Virginia), for example, bear 142 male and 16 female signatures, and 48 male and 29 female marks for the years 1693 to 1699; 161 male and 42 female signatures, and 16 male and 19 female marks for the years 1763 to 1771 (Cremin 1970, 533). This sample upholds an early estimation that in general about one of every three later colonial Virginia women could sign her name (Bruce 457). Documents from the backcountry of South Carolina reveal that 80 percent of males could sign their name (Cremin 1970, 543), and we may prudently suspect that the ability to write was also more prevalent among eighteenth-century southern women of English origin. It is difficult to draw conclusions from such figures, we should recall, because signatures exceed actual writing ability, especially for women. Moreover, aside from other factors (546-49), occasions for women to sign legal documents were far fewer than for men.

Were women in the southern colonies less literate than their northern contemporaries? They probably were during the seventeenth century and probably not as markedly, if at all, during the eighteenth century. Two facts are more important in surmising why so few records survive of early southern female authorship: there were far fewer women, as a presence, in the southern colonies, and the majority of these fewer women, often indentured, filled agricultural (field) rather than domestic roles in the tobacco economy of the South. This was certainly the case in Maryland, where immigrant men outnumbered women by as much as six to one and never less than three to one in the seventeenth century (Carr and Walsh 1979, 25-26). The economic and social context of these seventeenth-century women was not especially conducive to the acquisition of domestic skills (Brown 1996, 83), not to mention the mastery of writing. The education of the apprenticed and indentured in Virginia and North Carolina featured reading, rather than writing, though by the middle of the eighteenth century instruction in writing became more common, most notably in schools for girls (Spruill 1938, 186, 189, 202). In this regard, Elizabeth Sprigs's desperate letter to her angry father might be noteworthy (Calder 1935, 151-52), although this indentured servant in Maryland may have learned to read while a child in London and probably dictated her letter to someone else to pen. Usually, even when a woman of the southern colonies had the remainder of her indenture purchased by a husband, she often found herself subsequently performing field work as well as domestic chores (Carr and Walsh 1979, 41), which left little leisure for such activities as reading or writing.

To be sure, this is only a small part of *her-story* in the southern colonies, where from 1696 to 1776 at least five women were identified as printers (Hudak 1978). The pattern of signatures, at least, suggests that more women acquired literary skills as the population of this region transformed from an immigrant to a predominantly indigenous one during the eighteenth century. Up to the middle of this century, these women doubtless shared with their northern sisters, as recorded in Esther Edwards Burr's letter-journal, the onus of the prevailing social belief that writing as a leisure activity was not an appropriate or healthy undertaking for them. For most of these women, apparently, skill in writing was primarily intended for such occasions as signing their name, keeping domestic accounts, recording spiritual affections in a diary, or sending necessary notes or letters (such as ordering supplies).

The activity of reading itself was evidently not entirely exempt from similar concerns in the southern colonies during the eighteenth century. Pertinent here is Eliza Lucas Pinckney's record of her mother's fear (oddly reminiscent of Winthrop's diagnosis of Anne Yale Hopkins) that her daughter "shall read [herself] mad." Mrs. Pinckney had such "a great spite at [Eliza's] books" that she "had like to have thrown a volume of [her] Plutarchs lives into the fire" (Pinckney 1972, 33).

Other later southern women may have written more extensively than we know today, particularly among the Quakers. Such southern Quaker women as itinerant Sophia Wigington Hume (1701-74), author of the often reprinted *Exhortation to the Inhabitants of the Province of South-Carolina* (1747), tended (like their northern peers) to be more literate than average for their sex. Nevertheless, since southern women had far fewer opportunities than their northern sisters for their writings to be published, we know precious little about such activity.

Such details at least partially explain why southern women are virtually unrepresented in my study. It is also significant, in terms of my reliance on biblical allusion as the medium for measuring their peers' struggle with authority, that the culture of southern women was apparently characterized by a form of "desacralization." In comparison to England, that is to say, the culture of seventeenth-century Maryland and Virginia experienced a diminishment of the practice and influence of formal Christianity (Horn 1994, 400).

This process would likely explain why the extant writings of southern colonial women evince far fewer biblical allusions than do the documents left by their northern sisters.

Strangers in a Strange Land

Nevertheless, the details presently at hand pertaining to both the northern and southern colonies reinforce the impression, as given by Bradstreet's early concession that "Men can doe best, and Women know it well" (McElrath and Robb 1981, 7), that the ability to write was generally perceived as a male property. Colonial women must truly have had a different relationship to textuality (Miller 1986). Women, in London (Cole 1994) as well as in the New World, were a very limited presence among publishers, and of the twelve known colonial female printers (Hudak 1978) in the period covered by my study evidently only Ann Smith Franklin in Newport, Rhode Island, contributed to any publication, in this case a series of almanacs.

Female colonists did read works written by other women, as a recent study indicates (Hayes 1996), but most of the books they read were written by male authors—British poets Richard Blackmore (c. 1650-1729), Isaac Watts (1674-1748), and Edward Young (1683-1765) were favorites. This pattern did not significantly alter until well after the formation of the Republic. Although by the middle of the eighteenth century they were reading, among other female-authored works, *Poems* (1664) by Katherine Philips (a Welsh celebrant of female friendship), *Several Poems Compiled with Great Variety of Wit and Learning* (1678, 1758) by Anne Bradstreet (a colonial Congregationalist), *Poems on Several Occasions* (1696) and *Letters, Moral and Entertaining, in Prose and Verse* (1729-33) by Elizabeth Singer Rowe (an English religious author), and *Miscellanies in Prose and Verse* (1752) by Mary Jones (an English Deist), colonial women tended to feel excluded from the world of print. Pertinently Brewster lamented in 1757: "rare it is to see a Female Bard, / Or that my Sex in Print have e're appear'd" (2). Thirty-two years later during the early Republic, when some concern was expressed about the need for a suitable "republic of letters," a Mrs. Holmes in William Hill Brown's *The Power of Sympathy* (1789) complained (in a letter) that since "American literature boasts so few productions from the pens of ladies," women readers must necessarily rely on books written by men (61).

Given the pervasiveness of this perception and experience, colonial women who approached writing as an activity in itself were probably very self-conscious in their undertaking. The likelihood of such self-awareness at that time is suggested today by the example of a recent female Mennonite author, a member of the Old Order Amish preserving many of the Anabaptist beliefs and practices of their seventeenth-century Pennsylvania ancestors. In response to the sudden death of her son, Esther F. Smucker expressed her unauthorized protracted grief in a personal diary. Eventually three other women—her mother, her sister, and a neighbor—urged her to circulate this journal as a possible help to others, but Smucker hesitated for a long while over the prospect of publishing it. She worried specifically about the response of her Old Amish community to the book, not only its contents but also its very existence. The Mennonite community today, as in the past, frowns upon either an emphasis on earthly loss or a display of inner sentiment; and although Mennonite women are not forbidden to write, over the centuries very few have published because their community considers such activity as especially inappropriate for women, who ideally should be engaged in more worthwhile activities—child care, sewing, canning, and farm chores, for instance.

This latter-day instance of one Old Order Amish woman's extreme discomfort with authorship, grounded as it is in seventeenth-century Pennsylvania Mennonite tradition, intimates that in response to writing as an activity colonial women in general likewise experienced uncertainty in authorization. And this uncertainty was doubtless exacerbated by male control over both literary genres and scriptural allusions. Such control, in a tangential mode, is starkly evident in *A Confession of Faith*. Sarah Symmes Fiske (1652-92) wrote this little book when she was twenty-five years old and married, but (despite its utterly ordinary catechismal content) an authorizing male editor designated its printed version as primarily useful to "the Children of this Land" (2).

For nearly one hundred fifty years, in short, to a significant degree colonial women authors found themselves in foreign territory, unsettled strangers in a strange land. They replicated the precarious undertaking of their colonies, likewise marginalized and feminized by the homeland as they struggled for identity (Caldwell 1988; Cowell 1994, 115; Porterfield 1992, 143). But there was an important difference. Whereas the political and aesthetic features of colonial culture changed dramatically during these one and a half centuries, the predominant features of the colonial cultural definition of women essentially remained constant. Gains for women in several areas tended to be offset by losses in other areas. If as a group during the eighteenth century, for instance, women benefited from expanding opportunities to become fully literate, at the same time they suffered from declining opportunities to speak personally in colonial courts. During the preceding century, when lawyers were prohibited and rules were simplified in the colonial courts, Puritan women were encouraged to plead their own cases, and over 16 percent of them did so. This privilege contracted during the turn of the century, when more traditional English rules and practices invaded the colonial justice system. By the middle of the eighteenth century the public space of the courtroom became a masculine arena dominated by male legal professionals serving commercially active men. In cases involving fornication, for example, men were no longer judicially chastised alongside women, whose claims were now treated with skepticism but whose pregnancies certainly guaranteed their own legal prosecution (Dayton 1995, 16-68). Accordingly, female voices, however more literate at the time, faded into virtual silence within a jurisprudence that increasingly defined women as dependent, apolitical, and (in Cotton Mather's terms) an ornament of virtue.

As the case studies in my book demonstrate, too, whatever increasing liberalization colonial women experienced in their practical lives, their sense of themselves, their personal struggle with identity, remained disconcertingly consistent during the entire colonial period. Restricted to well before the post-Revolutionary economic changes that augmented extensive female literacy (Main 1991), emergent activism (Kelley 1992), and identification with history texts (Baym 1995, 1992)—not to mention such early national defenses of female education as the anonymous *Hapless Orphan* (1793) and Charles Brockden Brown's *Alcuin* (1798)—my book attempts to excavate several sites of logonomic conflict that disclose something of northeastern colonial American women's underground narrative within the prevailing ideological complex of their time.

Purview

Although I speak of these authors collectively, for the sake of economy of expression, I emphatically do not mean to suggest that every writing by a woman living in the colonial northeastern region of the American colonies necessarily reflects logonomic conflict. My argument applies to a representative group of works by female authors who, for various reasons, register logonomic conflict specifically in the application of *scriptural allusions*. My book, therefore, is selective in four ways.

First, given the presently known facts reviewed earlier in this chapter, southern women are virtually absent from my investigation. The writers featured in this book range in region from Vermont to Pennsylvania and New Jersey—a region given the convenient shorthand designation *northeastern* in my study—but my initial goal was to include southeastern women as well. I had hoped that they in particular would allow me to assess female Anglican and Roman Catholic responses along with the Congregational, Presbyterian, and Quaker examples from the northern and mid-Atlantic colonies.

My search for pre-Revolutionary southern women authors was frustrating, to say the least. Both *Intellectual Life in the Colonial*

South, 1585-1763 and *The History of Southern Literature* were not very helpful. Even more unexpected, only Eliza Lucas Pinckney was included in the massive biographical volumes of the classic *Library of Southern Literature,* which otherwise includes many now obscure later female writers. Pinckney appears briefly in chapter 2 of my study, but her letterbook, Martha Daniell Logan's gardening tract (1772), and Margaret Brett Kennett's letters on natural features (of which only excerpts are available)—all from eighteenth-century South Carolina, incidentally—offer insufficient evidence for observations about Anglican female authorship relative to my focus on logonomic conflict in the writings of their northern peers.

To date the most valuable resources for identifying southern female authors have been provided by Sharon M. Harris in a selective bibliography and an anthology of writings by early American women. Unfortunately, the southerners included in these two projects are a distinct minority, are often Quakers, and are more engaged by secular than by religious concerns. Ideally someone will unearth a cache of manuscripts by various colonial southern women and will write the chapters I reluctantly must forgo here. Perhaps then we will see whether scriptural allusions in writings by Anglican and Roman Catholic women evidence logonomic conflict in a manner similar to or different from the Congregationalist, Presbyterian, and Quaker instances reviewed in this book. That there may be a difference is suggested by a recent study of the life of Marie Guyart, a French nun in colonial Quebec whose spiritual relation (1654) (toned down in the posthumously published *La Vie de venerable Mere Marie de l'Incarnation* [1677]) records a mystical resolution of her discontents (Davis 1995, 101).

Second, my study also bypasses northern women writers who do not employ scriptural allusions, the matrix for my assessment of logonomic conflict, or who use such allusions only briefly and apparently without tension. Logonomic conflict, however, is not restricted to this matrix. It can be detected in colonial women's management of such other matrices as literary conventions.

Third, by accident, not by design, my investigation features personal narratives, including poems, memoirs, letters, and biblical paraphrases. Fiction is notably absent, though this omission had not been my intention. I had hoped, in fact, to include such an early novel as Frances Brooke's *The History of Emily Montague* (1769). Brooke was the daughter of an Anglican minister and married to another; her epistolary novel written in Quebec City specifically critiques the notion that "women are only born to suffer and to obey" (164); and one of the main correspondents in her work explicitly declares that she is "extremely religious" (93). Yet, only one muted biblical allusion emerges in the midst of a number of classical and Renaissance quotations in the novel.

Fourth, my book also omits women authors, particularly other Quakers and other former captives, whose work merely reinforces what has been already demonstrated in my presentation. My study, in short, is not designed to identify fully or to treat exhaustively early American female writers. The chapters of my report provide a "representative" record of women authors who register conflict in their application of scriptural authority to such personal concerns as identity, love, separation, fear, death, anger, subjection, freedom, and prospects.

In all but a very few instances, as a means of avoiding confusion with my own emphases, italic print has been deleted from quoted biblical and colonial American passages. I have used the King James version of the Bible throughout my discussion, save in my comments on Anne Bradstreet, who used the Geneva Bible. Although the King James translation appeared in 1611, it was not prominent in the northeastern colonies until much later in the seventeenth century.

Finally, the detection of logonomic conflict, similar to hesitating over the logogic crux, requires close attention to the text. To repeat a point from the precursor of this study, my method here endorses J. Hillis Miller's recent argument for an academic return to an awareness of the text as a text. Before introducing our students to the abstractions of literary theory, Miller urges, we should first undertake the "traditional task" of "the teaching of *reading*," of instruction "in reading all the signs" (1989, 102-11). In the course of my career, perhaps influenced by my training in science, I have remained convinced that if there is a "story," it will be unfolded through its details, its abundance of particulars. Exploring sites of logonomic conflict involves a sensitivity to detail and nuance, an alertness to even seemingly slight matters. For beneath these occasions, scarcely noticeable seismic activity may open small, albeit indicative, breaks in the apparently conventional surface and ingenuous associations of a writing. In such lacunae several northeastern colonial American women unwittingly found uncomfortable places to express their otherwise repressed personal response to theocratic authority.

ONE

～

Authority and Witchery

To begin this investigation with Cotton Mather (1663-1728) and
Mary English (1652?-94) is to begin with one of the most public
and one of the most obscure figures of colonial America. It is to
begin, in other words, with a metonymy of the theocratic textu-
alization of gender identity in the colonies. Mather and English are
representative figures. Their lives intersected during the Salem witch
trials, but of primary interest here is how both his book and her
poem were deformed by the logonomic conflicts endemic to their
mutually unstable attempt to negotiate an authorized identity for
women.

Cotton Mather's Manual for Women

Cotton Mather's *Ornaments for the Daughters of Zion* had at least
fifty years of currency in the marketplace. First printed in New England during the years 1691-92, a second edition was published in
London in 1694, and a third in Boston in 1741 (Holmes 1940,
2:774-76). Although Mather's book appeared during both the seventeenth and the eighteenth centuries, the two colonial editions
show no substantive differences (Cowell, intro. to Mather [1741]
1978, xix-xx). In the minds of some colonists, evidently, little had
changed concerning the place of women during those fifty years.

Mather intended this book "to advance Virtue among those, who
cannot forget their Ornaments, and yet often forget those Things
which are no less Necessary than Ornamental" (ii). This comment,
which displays the prevalent eighteenth-century understanding of

"ornament" as an adornment or embellishment that is more likely to be decorative than useful, suggests Mather's ambivalence toward his subject. His concern is not only that women seem to be fixated upon the ornaments of this world (including appearance and fashion) but also that women, as the second sex, seem themselves to be ornamental in the providential scheme. It was Eve's ornamental allure, male Puritan authorities deduced from Genesis, that had distracted Adam and led him and his posterity to death.

Acknowledging this cultural perception of women, Mather defends his undertaking against those who "Criminate an Undertaking to write a little Book for promoting the Fear of God in the Female Sex" (ii). Mather, as he says, restricts himself here to "a little Book," as if in some deference to the criticism he ostensibly resists. Does the brevity of his book unwittingly acknowledge a perceived problem with the comprehension of his declared audience, or does it obliquely concede the relative inconsequentiality of such a task devoted to women? To what extent does he unconsciously surmise that a volume directed to the ornamental sex, inherently fascinated by the ornaments of the material world, is itself ultimately only an ancillary ornament, at best only a similarly useful adjunct, within ecclesiastical discourse?

Before we investigate this conflicted state of mind represented in Mather's text, it is pertinent to observe a contextual matter. A pattern in Mather's printed funeral sermons from 1689 to 1728, roughly the same period of time spanned by the editions of *Ornaments,* helps illuminate this context. During this interval nearly half of Mather's funeral orations concern women, whereas 75 percent of his peers' published sermons concern men (Andrews 1970, 28). Pertinently, in *Ornaments* Mather records his awareness of the predominance of women over men in church attendance. "Indeed, there are more Women than Men, in the Church," he observes early in his discourse; later he likewise asserts, "there are far more godly Women in the World, than there are godly Men; and our Church Communions give us a little Demonstration of it. I have seen it without going a Mile from home, that in a Church of between three and four Hundred Communicants, there are but few more than one Hundred Men; all the rest are Women" (9, 48). Current historical investigations of church attendance records from 1660 onward substantiate Mather's sense of the steadily increasing feminization of the New England laity (Moran and Vinovskis 1992, 90-95; Porterfield 1992, 118).

It is probable that Mather's attention to women registers his desire to reclaim an ecclesiastical past that seemed to him to have ebbed during his own ministry. Behind this attention is a concern with "a fearful decay of Piety," which emerges like a refrain in his writings (Scheick 1989, 22-24). At a time when men seemed to be increasingly engaged in worldly rather than ecclesiastical affairs (Andrews 1970, 31), Mather apparently turned to his female parishioners in the hope of both stemming the tide of impiety and reclaiming his ministerial authority. As a descendent of the powerful Mather dynasty and as someone inordinately sensitive to any sign of his lessened role in secular and church affairs (Middlekauff 1971; Silverman 1984), however, Cotton admitted the necessity of shifting his attention to female piety in his own parish, albeit he did so with an undercurrent of anxiety. For given the secondary, adjunctive position of women in church and state affairs, defining his ministry primarily in terms of female laity would at some level of Mather's mind have readily augmented his sense of diminished personal efficacy. This necessitated alignment of the male ministry with female parishioners, a demographic feature of developing American church politics in general (Douglas 1977), evidently engendered a core of deep-seated ambivalence in Cotton Mather. And in these circumstances, as we will see, his expression of authority mimics the logonomic conflict evident in the writings of colonial women such as Mary English.

Mather's ambivalence, subtly negotiating his minced claim for female power and his ratification of personal power through this diminished claim, is evident throughout *Ornaments*. Designed to elevate the authority of women and thereby the authority of his own ministry increasingly identified with such female authority, the

argument of *Ornaments* is vexed whenever Mather's conscious sym-
pathetic affirmations are crossed by his unconscious antipathetic
denials of female power. This dualism is also evident in Mather's
progressive instruction of his daughters in both reading and writing (the latter not common at the time) coupled with his severe
restriction of the range and nature of their learning (Monaghan
1991). Mather can find little ground to empower women, as he
observes in one of his unpublished books (1726-27), where he
prophecies that in heaven women will shed their dubious temporal
gender and be restored to their radical Adamic nature: "the
Handmaids of the Lord, A REDEEMER who was once Born of a
Woman, intends unknown Dignities for you, and will make an Use
of you beyond what we yett know, to serve His Kingdome, when
[at the end of time] it shall cease to be with you as now it is, and
your Subjection to Men, shall with your Distinction from them,
no longer be considered" (Smolinski 1995, 266). Nevertheless,
Mather must credit women sooner rather than later if he is to rescue the times from impiety and his own ministry from being merely
ornamental, even if such an enablement of the second sex inherently raises questions about the status of the very male authority he
hopes to resuscitate in his own case.

The second paragraph of his discussion is indicative: "Tho' the
Apostle . . . gives the Prohibition so much Transgres'd by the most
Absurd Sect in our Days, That the Woman may not speak in the
Church; yet our God has employ'd man[y] Women to Write for
the Church, & Inspir'd some of them for the Writing of the Scriptures" (3). Mather refers to 1 Corinthians 14:34, where Saint Paul
admonishes: "Let your women keep silence in the churches: for it
is not permitted unto them to speak." Reinforced (as will be evident in English's poem) by the lesson of the "good part" allegorized
in Mary of Bethany's devoted silence at Jesus' feet (Luke 10:38-42;
Mather [1741] 1978, iii), this Pauline passage was experienced by
Puritan women as a testament to their lack of authorized speech in
both ecclesiastical and secular matters. That this interpretation was
still strong well into the eighteenth century is evident in a 1754

report by Esther Edwards Burr; she records one male's application of the insulting sobriquet "women popes" to several outspoken females who interfered in the selection of a new minister—a charge of subversion indeed, since (as Burr also reports) precisely at that time "popish enimies" were commonly associated with French militaristic "desighns" in the New World (Karlsen and Crumpacker 1984, 74, 76-77). Mather certainly follows this tradition when he employs this Pauline passage to rebuke female Quakers, "the most Absurd Sect in our Days" (3), just as Anne Hutchinson's accusers used it against her during the Antinomian crisis.

But something curious happens in Mather's sentence. Just as Anne Hutchinson retorted that elsewhere (Titus 23-25) Saint Paul sanctions the instruction of young women by older women, Mather points to noteworthy exceptions to Saint Paul's injunction. Mather's "yet" opens a space, especially when he proceeds to instate "man[y] Women" who have been divinely inspired to write on church matters. Mather's "yet," like Hutchinson's biblical counter, creates a bifurcation in authority; it points to an injunction applicable in one place and not in another. Surely some traditional biblical commentary is called for here to explain how such instances of exceptions to Pauline authority are authorized. But Mather silently allows his "yet," and the contraries it rhetorically hinges, to stand alone. He simply ignores this site of logonomic conflict, and the reader is left to negotiate the ellipsis.

A rift also emerges as Mather struggles to find female exemplars. He cites many but always only in passing. Often, in a contrary move, he must discount these models, at least to some extent, because they are either Old Testament or secular personages, and because in many instances they surpass the level of opportunity open to his audience. After one such long list, for example, he writes: "There is Wisdom in these Things; and the Women which have had it, are therefore to be praised. But, as the Apostle said, Yet I shew unto you a more excellent Way; so I say, there is a greater Wisdom than all of this" (37). What one hand grants out of the necessity of his argument, Mather's other hand takes away out of deference to

Pauline authority (1 Cor. 12:31). And like the "yet" in the previous passage, here the "but" alone tenuously spans two unexplained and apparently irreconcilable contentions.

Still more frequently, Mather refers to male authorities, whom he instates in his discussion by means of such compromising rhetorical maneuvers as "her Answer is in Words, like those that Joseph had unto his Brethren"; "she can say as Nehemiah did of old"; and "like David she must cry out of broken Bones" (25). Similar maneuvers are evident in Mather's management of what he refers to as requisite modifications of male models: for example, "it may with only the necessary Variation be said of her, as it was of Cornelius long ago," and "as the Almighty God was called, The Fear of Isaac . . . so may He be called, The Fear of the virtuous Woman" (27).

Perhaps if Mather had felt comfortable in highlighting the Virgin Mary as a model, he might have faired somewhat better in his search for prototypes. Bridget Richardson Fletcher (1726-70), of uncertain religious background, seized such an opportunity in a private hymn:

> What man is there, that shall thus dare
>   Woman to treat with scorn,
> Since God's own son, from heav'n did come,
>   Of such an one was born. [Cowell 1981, 250]

And Jane Colman Turell, praising English poet Elizabeth Singer Rowe, in 1725, applies an allusion that was generally interpreted as a prophecy of Mary's divine role: "A Woman's Pen strikes the curs'd Serpents Head, / And lays the Monster gasping, if not dead" (Turell 1735, 73).

Calvinists, however, more generally believed (as Cotton Mather indicates in *Ornaments*) that the "Blessed Virgin" had become "to Popish Idolaters" an icon of "Mediation and Intercession" worshipped with a cultlike adoration appropriate to the deity alone (2). So Mather barely mentions her in passing. With (as he says) safety in mind, the best he can say about Mary, it seems, is rather tepid and hesitant. In his quick observation that "we may safely account the Female Sex herein [in Mary] more than a little dignified" (2-3), the nearly oxymoronic phrase "more than a little" intimates Mather's discomfort with the mother of Jesus, a traditional Protestant discomfort that has been interpreted in later times as a fear of feminine identity (Ong 1967, 193).

In reflecting on the fact that the Redeemer "was Born of a Woman" (3), Mather reinscribes William Ames's similar maneuver (Thickstun 1988, 9) of shifting to the figure of Eve. Eve, not Mary, is the traditional Calvinistic model for defining female identity: "As a Woman had the Disgrace to go first in that horrid and wo[e]ful Transgression of our first Parents, which has been the Parent of all our Misery; so a Woman had the Glory of bringing into the World that Second Adam, who is the Father of all our Happiness" (1-2). For Mather, Mary is less a person in her own right than an antitype for Eve. The figure of Eve lies, like a palimpsest, beneath Mary's identity. Mather's focus on Eve, accordingly, provides another site of logonomic conflict in his discourse, which attempts (without directly encountering the matter) to empower women through Eve, the very figure of female disempowerment.

Mather seeks to empower women by indicating that Eve's position as the mother of humanity is a divinely ennobled female heritage. This aspect of his argument reaches an apogee of sorts when he declares, in the situational terms of his ministerial needs, "It is indeed a Piece of great Injustice, that every Woman should be so far an Eve, as that her Depravation should be imputed unto all the Sex" (54). But the negative element embedded in this otherwise worthy sentiment is not merely latent; its residual power had in fact more forcefully emerged two pages earlier in Mather's book, where an antipathetic and scripturally authorized claim is asserted: "It is mention'd as the singular Unhappiness of Women, in 2 Tim. 3.6 . . . [that] the weaker Sex, who are most easily gained themselves [by devil-like seducers of mind and body], and then fit Instruments for the gaining of their Husbands, to such Errors as cause them to lose their Souls at last" (52). Women, in other words, are still Eves today, not only as life-giving mothers but also *singularly* as death-engendering agents of postlapsarian mortality and spiritual fatality.

Mather's double-voiced suggestion that each woman should identify with the honorable status of "her first Mother" and, at the same time, "recover [her] impaired Reputation" (20, 46) amounts to a tug-of-war between contrary impulses in his book. This unresolved contest is mirrored in the general statements about women scattered throughout *Ornaments*. On the one hand, for instance, Mather assails "the petulant Pens of some froward and morose Men, [who] have sometimes treated the Female Sex with very great Indignities" in "whole Volumns . . . written, to disgrace that Sex, as if it were . . . The meer Confusion of Mankind" and as if "No Woman is good" (46). On the other hand, Mather elsewhere unthinkingly joins ranks with these very men when he proclaims that women are prone to "deceive unwary Men, into those Amours which bewitching Looks & Smiles do often betray the Children of Men"; that "the Female Sex is naturally the fearful Sex" as a result of the Fall; that women are much harder to rescue "from the Snares of Whoredom" than are men; and that "the Female Sex is doom'd" to endure "the Curse in the Difficulties both of Subjection and of Childbearing" (11, 20, 48). "It seems," Mather reassures his readers, that the "Chains" and "Pains" of the curse on women have "been turn'd into a Blessing" (48); but the word "seems" here once again registers an uncertainty in the conflicted voice in *Ornaments,* an unwitting hesitation that equivocates and potentially subverts its ostensible reassurance.

In its clearest moments, Mather's book instructs women to accept, in utter obedience, their obligatory subjugation to the deity and his male minions on earth. In Puritan culture, the "weaker sex" was both morally and civilly bound by this dual requirement (Ulrich 1982, 6-7, 107-8). Women, Mather therefore counsels, should respond to God's summons like Abigail to David's, like the Virgin Mary to the angel Gabriel (40), and perhaps like Mather's wife

(Abigail) to Cotton. Abigail's reply foreshadows the Virgin Mary's response to the angel's announcement that she is to become the mother of Jesus: "Behold the handmaid of the Lord; be it unto me according to thy word" (Luke 10:38). When "our heavenly David, sends to marry your Souls unto himself," Mather instructs his female audience, imitate Abigail: "She bowed her self on her Face to the Earth, and said, behold, let thine Handmaid, be a Servant, to wash the Feet of the Servants of my Lord" (77). So, too, ideally each wife "ever treats him [her husband] with the Language of an Abigail" (90).

This paradigm of Abigail's obedience, however, is highly problematical on at least two counts. First, it repositions women precisely in the diminutive place of disempowerment from which Mather attempts to elevate both them and his own seemingly diminished ministry over an increasingly female laity. Mather's advice, in effect, reinforces Saint Paul's pronouncement that "women keep silence in the churches: for it is not permitted unto them to speak," a pronouncement Mather initially tried to qualify through a strategic rhetorical ellipsis. Second, while the analogy of the husband in Abigail's example certainly instructs women to obedience to God and to his ministerial ambassadors, it also necessarily consigns these women to an unequivocal subordination to the very husbands who (as we noted) are increasingly outside the reach of the church in general and Mather in particular.

The work of a man sensitive to his decreasing capacity to contain impiety in male-dominated public affairs, *Ornaments* is to a significant extent ambivalently devoted to shifting the basis of Mather's power to a "diminutive" second sex ideally obedient to his pastoral oversight. Reflecting Mather's conflicted attempt to enhance women's province and at least to some degree reclaim his own seemingly diminished voice, *Ornaments* fissures in various places as a result of its underground seismic problem with authorization. The problematic defense of women's identity in Mather's "little Book" is thoroughly riddled by unnegotiated and unredeemed bifurcations similar to those in the conflicted search for authorized voice evident in writings by Mary English and other seventeenth-century Puritan female authors.

Mary English's Acrostic

Not generally known for the single poem of hers that has survived, Mary English is remembered as a participant in the Salem witch trials and as an ancestor of Nathaniel Hawthorne. In 1692, she was imprisoned for at least six weeks on the charge, as phrased in the warrant for her arrest, of "high Suspition of Sundry acts of Witchcraft done or Committed . . . Lately upon the Bodys of Anna Putnam & Mercy Lewis" (Boyer and Nissenbaum 1974, 805). Having forfeited their ample estate and later aided by friends, Mary and her Huguenot husband Philip, also accused of witchcraft, both escaped execution by fleeing to New York, where Mary died in 1694.

We know very little about the details of her indictment. Virtually all of the papers relating to her examination have disappeared (Cheever 1860, 243), allowing her to elude us today as she did her accusers then. We do know that in one of the Salem trial papers Mercy Lewis specifically claimed not only that Mary had threatened to "Afflict [Mercy] Dreadfully & kill" her if she did not "set [her] hand to a Booke," but also that in the presence of the grand jury Mary's shape had stroked Mercy's breast and choked her to prevent her testimony (Boyer and Nissenbaum 1974, 319). And in another deposition Susannah Sheldon insisted that she had been bitten by Mary, who at the time bore the image of a yellow bird on her breast (105).

Even if perchance Mary English had been personally involved in some form of natural magic or had merely associated with people who dabbled in the practice in some manner, she would simply have been encountering a common feature of the popular culture of her day. Because of the stormy events surrounding the Salem witch trials, it is easy for us to overlook the fact that in Mary English's time interest in the supernatural was not confined to a Christian context. Puritans brought with them British lore and superstitions (Yates 1979, 177-81), a long-lived medieval and Renaissance fascination with the occult sciences. Moreover, the alchemical studies of such New Englanders as George Starkey and John Winthrop the Younger derived from contemporary progressive English and Continental "scientific" thought, which credited dreams, revelations, and intuitions (Newman 1994).

Besides clerically authored books on various wonders in the visible world, for example, Anne Bradstreet's verse demonstrates her comfortable appropriation of imagery relating to alchemical transformation (Rosenmeier 1991, 52-55), Cotton Mather's writings record his keen interest in astrology (Winship 1990), and Edward Taylor's poetry characteristically refers to both alchemical processes and curses, including "strange and bewitching spells" ("Meditation 2.3" [Stanford 1960, 85]). Of course, such occurrences in Puritan writings were Christianized—Christ's alchemy redeems demonic wizardry and Christ's grace dispels Satan's curses. Nevertheless, within the drama of this spelling and dispelling, pagan beliefs provided an enduring subtextual context and, as a result, maintained a covert existence (like a palimpsest) beneath the Christian overlay of Puritan attitudes. The debris of these decaying systems of belief was present in daily life (Hall 1989, 71-103), as well, whenever Puritans resorted (as some people still do today) to little superstitious acts to ward off bad luck (as in the colonial practice of boiling hair and urine), to forecast the future (as in the colonial practice of peering into egg whites), or to inquire of the dead (as in the colonial practice of turning a sieve while ritualistically invoking Saint Peter and Saint Paul). An understructure of hermetical and occult beliefs survived within Puritan culture just as they have within Christianity in general. Such a heritage can be seen in our own time in amalgamations like Mexican Catholicism or whenever someone routinely knocks on wood or tosses a pinch of salt over a shoulder.

It is important to remember, too, that the superstitious beliefs and behavior Puritans ordinarily encountered in their daily lives were not experienced as demonic witchcraft. The term "witchcraft" is not clearly defined in the King James version of the Bible, although this translation reflects the British sovereign's personal interest in demonology (Starkey 1949, 37). And, as Cotton Mather reported, maleficent magic was uncommon; its alleged incidence was often the product of "abusive Tongues" or rumors that "traduce for a Witch, every old Woman, whose Temper with her Visage is not eminently good" (115). Age, particularly when associated with lost fertility, evidently was a factor in these rumors, for alleged witches frequently were women at the age of menopause or women without children, which related them to menopausal women (Berkin 1996, 47). These conditions were natural, of course, but they nonetheless reduced the social status of menopausal and childless women, and also made them vulnerable to various social anxieties concerning unnaturalness as if they embodied a malign inversion of the proper order of things. Puritan folk, however, customarily regarded natural magic as basically benign (Weisman 1984, 41-42), as chiefly a matter of warding off, curing, or furthering. Familiar Puritan superstitious practices, moreover, frequently featured medical cures and drew upon botanical folklore.

Such small gestures did not much disturb the clergy, who definitely knew about them. Ministers denounced such behavior when it seemed to exceed some undeclared boundary, a pattern that intensified in the course of the century as the clergy became anxious over the diminishment of New England's spiritual prospects and of their own spiritual leadership (Godbeer 1992, 84). This boundary remained variable because there was an uncertain distinction between "folkloric beliefs incorporated into religious culture by clergymen and layfolk and those specifically magical traditions that ministers and the more exclusivist of their flock condemned as contravening reformed theology" (16). It is pertinent to note, for our purposes, that the witchcraft scare in Salem specifically featured malevolent effects, such as deformities in body, mind, and behavior. Doubtless these perceived malignant consequences, not ordinary natural magic per se, fueled the trials, along with all the other likely social and interpersonal explanations reasonably advanced by recent scholars (e.g., Boyer and Nissenbaum 1974; Rosenthal 1993). And doubtless, too, this evidence of the potentially dark underside of folkloric customs now brought concerns to the foreground of authoritarian consciousness that previously had seemed important only sporadically.

Puritan authorities evidently had ignored the everyday minor superstitious behavior of the folk as a harmless and powerless practice, especially since the primary conservators of these customs were women (Koehler 1980, 276-81), the second-class citizens of the Puritan state who were popularly associated with witchcraft in both England and the colonies (Kern 1993). (Men were a distinct minority in this pursuit, and women—akin to Eve at the time of her fall—seemed to colonial justices to be more vulnerable than men to Satan's wiles [Dayton 1995, 32].) Beneficent conjuring, such as the use of charms to further romance or fertility, was condescendingly designated, by the male elite at least, as an innocuous, perhaps frivolous folk pursuit. Some of this older heritage of white magic mingled with the female practice of midwifery, which likewise was culturally relegated to a secondary position, particularly when compared with the Galenic medical training of male doctors. Indeed, the earliest accused witches in New England included herb-healers and midwives (Koehler 1980, 474). It may be noteworthy, in this regard, that the charges against Mary English specifically allude to medicinal witchery: "mrs english in the morning . . . told mee i should not eat no vittals"; "Mrs English . . . told mee . . . if I would but touch the Booke I should bee well, or else I should never" (Boyer and Nissenbaum 1977, 105, 319). The widespread tolerance of English's andro-centric culture toward such prescriptions in other contexts, a tolerance that included physicians' scholarly interest in natural magic (Watson 1991, 114-16) and ministers' habitual inclusion of folkloric notions in sermonic discourses (Hall 1989, 103-14), in effect authorized therapeutic conjuring as a mainly safe (that is, socially irrelevant) reservation for containing and displacing female power.

But as the episode in Salem in 1692 startlingly reminded, the threat of transgression was ever latent. This threat was specifically apparent in witches' language (Kamensky 1992), but men such as Cotton Mather were more generally alert to the power of women's "*bewitching* Looks & Smiles" to "often betray" and "deceive unwary Men" ([1741] 1978, 11; emphasis added); and men like John Winthrop had suspected that the practices of midwives were particularly prone to exceed minor superstitions and to utilize black magic ([1908] 1959, 1:266-68). Their concerns were nurtured by infrequent instances of women who had crossed the sanctioned perimeter of their preserve. When, for example, Margaret Jones of Charlestown did not merely ply her trade as folk healer but also bluntly assailed the authority of male doctors, she was executed as a witch in 1648; according to her indictment, she had asserted that "such as would not make use of her physic . . . would never be healed, and accordingly their diseases and hurts continued, with relapse against the ordinary course, and beyond the apprehension of all physicians and surgeons" (Hall 1989, 99). Such occasional earlier northeastern colonial prosecutions of witches and even the trouble with women during the antinomian crisis in 1637 notwithstanding, the events in Salem were unusually dramatic in indicating the degree to which "female witchery" could breach the containing boundaries of its socially defined reservation.

These events fostered a governmental attempt to reestablish this boundary because they demonstrated too palpably that representatives of the second sex who crossed the borders of their allotted place could betray, disrupt, and bewitch the social order outside their secondary preserve. In the Salem incident, for example, health, prayer, speech, and family duties were disrupted in the course of the afflicted young women's rebellion against whatever restrictions adult society routinely placed upon them. Given these signs of violation of the natural and social order, it is no wonder that one attending physician declared that the evil hand was upon them. To the Salem judges, as well, it must have seemed that disobedient Eve was loose again and this time about to wreak havoc in the New World.

Mary English seems to have been aware of women's capacity to contravene the restrictions placed upon them. And she seems to have perceived this potentiality in terms of female witchery, a power (as we noted) readily imputed to women by Cotton Mather and Puritan culture. A clue to this awareness is embedded in her verse acrostic, a poem in which the first letter of each line, read sequentially, spells the author's name.

We know very little about this undated poem. Was this apparently adult production (Cheever 1859, 164) written before, during, or after her Salem ordeal? Were we able to establish that this verse was composed before her imprisonment, we might have a special glimpse at her awareness of and possible attraction to therapeutic magic before the trials. But regardless of when she penned it, her acrostic is valuable for its record of English's divided sensibility concerning female witchery and cultural authority. Her undated poem reads:

> May I with Mary choose the better part
> And serve the Lord with all my heart,
> Receive his word most joyfully
> Y live to him eternally.
>
> Everliving God I pray,
> Never leave me for to stray;
> Give me grace thee to obey.
> Lord grant that I may happy be
> In Jesus Christ eternally.
> Save me dear Lord by thy rich grace;
> Heaven then shall be my dwelling place.
> [Cowell 1981, 202]

On its face, this verse is conventional, even cliché-ridden. The first line alone echoes a standard refrain concerning a Puritan woman's ideal disposition. On the first page of Cotton Mather's *Ornaments* "what Mary Chose"—"The good Part"—is applied to all women. The same allusion occurs, typically, in *Copy of a Valedictory and Monitory Writing* (1681), a prose consolation written by Sarah

Goodhue (1641-81) shortly before her death. Goodhue hoped that her daughter "with Mary . . . mayst find [she] hast chosen the better part" (Cowell 1981, 196). In English's verse, however, this biblical allusion warrants further consideration.

Luke (10:38-42) reports Jesus' visit at the home of Martha and Mary, the two sisters of Lazarus of Bethany. While Martha ceaselessly pursues the task of entertaining the visitor, her sister merely sits attentively at his feet. To her complaint that Mary has left her to do all the serving and to her request that the guest command her sister to help, Jesus replies that only "one thing is needful: and Mary hath chosen that good part."

Matthew Henry's *Commentary on the Whole Bible,* among other scriptural exegeses, interprets the episode of the two sisters as an allegory heuristically opposing Mary's sanctioned piety to Martha's unsanctioned dutiful action. As these commentaries suggest, compared to Martha's oversolicitous activity, Mary's devout submission (like the Virgin Mary's [Thickstun 1988, 8-9]) is the better part. To Congregationalists like Cotton Mather and Mary English, this scriptural passage describes the utter powerlessness of the soul before the deity's arbitrary, predetermined election of saints. As the Protestant commentaries suggest, justification (faith as represented by Mary's passive reception of the divine word) precedes sanctification (good works as represented by Martha's exertions on behalf of her divine guest). No activity, however pious, can merit or compare to saving faith.

Given this standard contemporary Reformed understanding of the Mary and Martha story, the turn of English's second stanza is as curious as are the conjunctions "but" and "yet" that we observed in Mather's *Ornaments.* English's second stanza focuses on action, but not on potentially sanctified action, which is what one might expect to follow from the poet's opening attempt to identify with Mary's justified faith. The second stanza features instead a request for divine help with such apparently unsanctified behavior as straying and disobedience. This shift, and its intimation of some aberrance, is reinforced by a drastic prosodic alteration in the second movement of her poem; whereas the first stanza is expressed in perfect iambs softly culminating in two rhymed pyrrhics, such harmonious order disintegrates into prosodic chaos in the second stanza. This characteristic of English's supplication inadvertently suggests the presence of some personal problem with obedience, in need of gracious redress, that already separates her from the ideal represented by Mary.

The movement of English's verse toward the question of obedience, moreover, is not authorized by standard Protestant commentaries on the passage from Luke. They explicitly indicate that obedience is not the point of this New Testament episode. Obedience is not addressed because Jesus gave Mary of Bethany no orders and specifically rebuked Martha for asking him to command her sister to some action. Mary simply "sat at Jesus' feet, and heard his word" (Luke 10:39). Mary obeys by hearing, which is to say that she is pious and devout through an inward faith far beyond conscious obedience. She, to apply English's words, "serve[s] the Lord with all [her] heart," rather than (like Martha) through the dutiful service of her actions. Indeed, in fundamental Calvinistic terms, self-conscious obedience is no better than Martha's oversolicitude; good works do not lead to or further justification.

The turn in the acrostic to the need for obedience, with its departure from Reformed scriptural exegesis and its prosodic insinuation of some resistant problem, is a rare reflection of English's self-awareness. Family tradition maintained, in fact, that she was routinely composed, aristocratic, and firm in character (Cheever 1860, 244). She was remembered, that is to say, as a woman with a secure sense of herself, a woman who may have been perceived by some of her contemporaries as inappropriately strong-willed. Pertinently, in the only surviving sheet among the Salem trial papers bearing her signature, English succinctly and forthrightly testified that she had heard young Mary Warren say that her two allegedly afflicted friends—the primary accusers of the alleged witches—were mere dissemblers, that "the Majestrats-might as well-Examen Keysers-Daughter that had bene Distracted many-years" (Boyer and

Nissenbaum 1977, 803). Without a trace of defensiveness, English ratifies Warren's revelation at a time when it was distinctly dangerous for her to be so assertive.

This characteristic firmness apparently informs English's intimation of an incongruity between her and Mary. In asking for remediation, the poet unwittingly directs her spiritual meditation away from the issue of justification toward a secular province of behavior that suggests a lack of saving faith. But why, we might wonder, is her meditation on faith, on election, distorted by this concern with straying through disobedience, a secular consideration disallowed by scriptural commentaries on the Luke passage and inimical to the poet's initial intention in her poem?

One answer may be that whereas the Reformed biblical exegetes applied the Mary and Martha story to everyone, Puritan ministers applied it to women. This is evident in Mather's opening comment in *Ornaments,* and that female parishioners followed suit is evident in English's and Goodhue's writings. This maneuver might have been less a problem in itself had not the ministry on related occasions correlated female spiritual justification and female social behavior. As Mather's *Ornaments* equivocally indicates, ministers did not stress only women's obedience to God the Father; they also emphasized, as a sanctified sign of justification, women's submission to familial, ecclesiastical, and societal fathers.

Congregationalist women like English were instructed, in terms of the Pauline epistles, that in the divine scheme women were naturally and spiritually subordinate to men, a position manifestly clear in the universal consequences of Eve's disobedience. In *Ornaments,* as we saw, Mather typically referred to the chief of these consequences as "the Curse . . . of Subjection . . . which the Female Sex is doom'd unto," a debility redressed when, with "perfect Obedience," a "Wife shines with the Husband's Rays" (39-40, 48). This context underlay English's attempt at a meditation on faith and her antithetical shift to unsanctified conduct, specifically some personal problem with insubordination. We should not lose sight of the force of this social or secular concern because English could not lose sight of it.

We will probably never know precisely what network of problems English may have had in mind when she wrote of her need for special help with straying through disobedience. But we do know about her strength of character and her indictment for witchcraft, an indictment that certainly combined secular and spiritual issues. We also know that women's unofficially licensed participation within the preserve of therapeutic charms and spells expressed their sense of power and that, by Mather's own admission, some women complained of male restrictions on their activities. And we know, as the Salem spectacle exhibited, that some women *may* have been tempted to expand their power beyond the societal limits placed upon it (Kibbey 1982), expand it most insubordinately in a necromantic direction contravening ministerial Christian authority.

Was Mary English tempted to defend therapeutic witchery, the preserve culturally allotted to women, even while she conceded its immanent transgressiveness? There is a hint in her poem—and it makes no difference in this regard whether it was written before, during, or after the Salem trials—that she might have been attracted to this traditional locus of female authority and (at least in her acrostic) might have worried about its dire spiritual and secular consequences for her. The hint emerges if we detect another biblical allusion well known to Puritans, an oblique allusion more appropriate to the consideration of obedience in English's acrostic than is the passage from Luke.

In writing "May I with Mary choose the better part / And serve the Lord with all my heart," English appears to have also thought of an Old Testament passage that can be related to the New Testament story of Mary and Martha. The passage reads: "Hath the Lord as great delight in burnt offerings and sacrifices, as in obeying the voice of the Lord?" (1 Sam. 15:22). Just as Jesus indicts Martha's dutiful activity as not the good part when compared with Mary's attentive hearing of the divine word, so too Samuel denounces Saul's active conformity to ceremonial observances as less valuable than complete submissive obedience to (or the *hearing* of) the voice of God: "Behold, to obey is better than sacrifice" (15:22).

In his catechism and elsewhere, Calvin indicates that this passage insists upon our absolute obedience to divine law (Reid 1954, 119, 229), and in his popular *The Day of Doom* Michael Wigglesworth explicitly interprets this passage to refer to the "perfect Obedience" that characterizes justification—the unmitigated hearing of the divine word that precedes "good works" or sacrifices (Bosco 1989, 34). This reading of the passage from Samuel is likewise explicit in *An Alarm Sounded to Prepare the Inhabitants of the World to Meet the Lord in the Way of His Judgment* (1709, 8), an autobiographical "little appearance" (4) by Bathsheba Bowers (c. 1672-1718), who was born in Massachusetts, raised in Pennsylvania, and preached Quaker doctrine in South Carolina. Puritans and Quakers, in short, read the Samuel episode as scriptural instruction about justification, just as biblical exegetes read the Luke episode. Puritan ministers also spoke of justification as absolute obedience to God. But this association of justification and "perfect Obedience" to the divine father (as evident in Wigglesworth's poem) was angled, in a manner unauthorized by scriptural exegetes, when (as is evident in Mather's book) ministers further suggested that "perfect Obedience" to human father figures was a particular sign of women's divine justification.

So although the commentaries do not link the Samuel and Luke episodes, English could easily align them because Puritan ministers read both of these biblical passages as instruction on justification by faith alone. Furthermore, as we noted, the clergy correlated justification and obedience in the Samuel passage as well as generally equated female redemption and female submission to secular authority. This associative context informs English's incidental departure from exegetical readings of the Luke passage when she veers away from Mary as gracious prototype and toward herself as possibly an insubordinate secular antithesis to such a model.

Enmeshed in this associative net, the word "better" in English's acrostic is allusively unstable and becomes a site of logonomic conflict similar to the term "ornaments" in Mather's book. The word "better," like the word "obey" later in the poem, literally appears in the passage in Samuel; but it is also the word traditionally substituted for "good" in allusions, like English's and Goodhue's, to the passage in Luke. The two allusions, and the clerical identification of them with justification, strategically intersect in this word. And this slippery transition between the evident allusion to Luke and the cloaked allusion to Samuel is especially interesting because it may provide a specific personal clue to the disjunctive shift of perspective in English's poem from spiritual meditation to a resistant secular problem. The cloaked biblical allusion may hint at the secret preserve of English's fear of straying from God through disobedience in the world. For in the Old Testament passage under consideration, Samuel explicitly correlates disobedience with witchcraft: "To obey is better than sacrifice. . . . For rebellion is as the sin of witchcraft, and stubbornness is as iniquity and idolatry" (15:22-23).

Disobedience, says judge Samuel, is akin to witchcraft; witchcraft, say English's Salem judges, is a form of disobedience, to the deity and to his male representatives. As characterized by the passage from Samuel, such rebellion, always a temptation within the preserve of female conjuring, is a form of prideful self-idolatry. To assert authority within this preserve is potentially to make a false god of oneself; it is potentially to repeat the sin of Eve's insubordination in proudly desiring to "be as gods" (Gen. 3:5). And similarly in English's acrostic, some insinuated locus of female *authority* and *action* in the secular world, such as witchcraft, emerges as a potential deauthorization of the poet's identification with Mary. In her poem this locus is a space of potentially transgressive behavior resisting her meditation on transcendent faith. English's verse suggests that she has had to choose between two dominions and that she has consciously tried to choose subordination to theocratic jurisdiction because, as a female, her submission to this secular authority would be a hopeful sign of her justified obedience to divine authority.

Nevertheless, her fear of straying, her fear of rebelliousness and possibly its biblical correlative witchcraft, is not quelled by her decision to submit. Her poem expressly indicates that she continues to worry about her own renitence. She experiences, in short, a divided sensibility that diverges sharply from Mary's example. Entangled in the ministerial association of female submission to God and female subordination to men, English is unable to negotiate her longing to acquiesce spiritually to scriptural authority and her lingering reluctance to acquiesce secularly to cultural authority. This experienced division between spiritual and secular authority, akin to Mather's elliptical coalescence of quotidian necessity and divine mandate, is represented by the gap between Mary's example and her own.

In one sense, English's divided sensibility is a concession to the ministerial insistence upon women's transference of "perfect obedience" to God to "perfect Obedience" to man. In other words, the poet's conscious desire to conform to the ministerial ideal precariously bridges the two parts and perspectives of her poem. In another sense, however, her divided sensibility unconsciously insists upon the separation of these two parts and perspectives. This underlying insistence in effect resists the unauthorized ministerial intersection of the spiritual and the secular with regard to female obedience. But such resistance is only *in effect*. Her milieu's coalescence of obedience to deity and man as the standard for female behavior leaves English bereft of a licensed means of negotiating the secular anxiety rubbing against the grain of her spiritual desire for the pristine attentiveness of Mary of Bethany. The tension wrought by English's effort to set aside the temptation of some disfranchised expression of female authority results in a bifurcated poem.

And might we not also wonder whether English's attraction to the acrostic as a form likewise latently conveys a hint of bifurcating resistance? Although Cotton Mather shows no interest in the form (Knight 1989), other Puritans appreciated their cultural inheritance of the acrostic genre, the uncertain heritage of which included its use in necromantic charms. The design of the acrostic is similar to the form of some magical spells of English's day. In a sense, English's poem appears to be one kind of spell designed to dispel another. Specifically, her acrostic reads as a formulary incantation devised to ward off the evil attraction of disobedience, which the Samuel passage equates to witchcraft. This association of official prayer and unsanctioned conjuring within the very form of her acrostic may be one more rift in the poem, one more sign of how a preserve of female power, or witchery, secretly resists from deep within the culturally authorized context of English's poem.

As we have seen, this bifurcating resistance is registered in the tension between an explicit allusion to Luke and an oblique allusion to Samuel; an attempted identification with Mary of Bethany and an unsanctified personal experience averting this identification; a desire for transcendent faith and a disqualifying fear of secular disobedience; a celebration of passive piety and a contrary active resolve to accept submission; a conscious acceptance of divine authority and an unconscious witchlike resistance to cultural authority; and an official prayer and an unsanctioned conjuration. In apparently moving from the allusion to Luke to the allusion to Samuel, moreover, English's poem even reverses the customary homiletic sequence in Puritan writing, which (as demonstrated in Edward Taylor's meditations) usually proceeds from the Old Testament to the New Testament. As all of these discordant features suggest, the disobedience, the witchery of female identity that Mary English wishes to disown, asserts itself against her will and deforms her poem, just as Cotton Mather's conflicted attempt to authorize women's social station and his own seemingly "feminized" ministry mars *Ornaments*.

English desires to renounce the marginalized preserve of female power (disobedience/witchery). Nevertheless, she cannot successfully negotiate the uneasiness emanating from her unwitting impulse to separate scriptural authority from secular authority, an impulse frustrated by a cultural hegemony that insistently coalesces these two authorities concerning women, even to the point of exceeding exegetical authority. The rifts in her verse signify an unconscious insurgency opposing her conscious effort to accept the cultural association of "perfect Obedience" in her secular affairs as a temporal sign of her spiritual condition. In fact, the tensions in her verse ultimately problematize any certain conclusion concerning whether assertive witchery or repressive authority is "the better part" for women to endorse.

The female authorization of Mary English's voice may have been disfranchised by the poet, her judges, and her social milieu, but it could not be silenced. In effect, it whispers a secret related to Mather's concern with the power of women's "bewitching Looks & Smiles"—the secret of the poet's unacknowledged and resistant attraction to disobedience and possibly its biblical and cultural correlative, witchcraft.

TWO

~

Love and Anger

Love was not exempt from the purview of colonial theocratic authority. This oversight was especially true in the Puritan settlements, where admonitions concerning excessive attachment to another person were common. It is in this environment that Jane Colman Turell typically worried about her feelings for Samuel, her only surviving offspring: "It may be I have made this Child too much an Idol" (Turell 1735, 107). But, if the letter-book of Eliza Lucas Pinckney (c. 1722-93) is representative, such concerns evidently occurred as well in southern Anglican communities. Pinckney writes, "We are not to fix our happiness on any thing beneath the supream Good nor Idolize the best man on Earth, or pay dearly for it" (140). Pinckney's northern female peers express precisely the same sentiment in response to the actual or imagined death of someone very dear to them, but in the context of the intense iconoclasm of the Puritan *mentalité* (Gilman 1986) their language is much less composed, much more anxious below its surface.

Pinckney wrote about idolizing men during her nearly two-year period of grief over the death of her husband. Her letter-book leaves no doubt about the depth of her sorrow; between July 1758 and March 1760, her letters not only refer to tearful nights but also sometimes temporarily cease when their author weeps too much while remembering her husband. And her letter-book leaves no doubt about the genuineness of her religious convictions; for from 1739 to 1762, her letters often refer to one's "duty to [the] Creator," including "an early piety and steady Virtue" (Pinckney 1972, 17). What separates Pinckney from her northern peers is the degree of intensity in reconciling "so severe a tryal" as her personal loss and "resignation to the Will of the All Wise disposer of Events, which was [her] indispensible duty as a Christian" (127).

Pinckney confesses her difficulty in forging this reconciliation. She admits how "hard [is] the task" of "resignation and submission which becomes [the] creature and servant" of "Great God Almighty," "how little" has been her "fortitude and Xian resolution" (102, 116). Despite this candid admission, however, no explicit or implicit sign of distortion occurs in her language. Her rationality parallels her grief, the very rationality that Pinckney time and again identifies as "the noblest principle of [human] nature" and of Christian belief (29, 46). As a student of "that admirable Author" John Locke (48), as someone well educated (in England) and widely read, Pinckney weathers her grief with the unshakable conviction that "to live agreeably" requires an adherence "to the dictates of reason and religion" (51). She experienced a struggle during those two years of mourning, but she succeeded in balancing reason and sorrow.

Aiding her during this time, as her letters also indicate, was a firm sense of the interrelation of the secular (rational thought) and the divine (religious belief), short of the excess of idolatry, of course. This sense was, in general, much more prevalent in Anglican than in Puritan religious practice. In Frances Brooke's contemporary *The History of Emily Montague* (1769), for example, the equation of rationality and religion informs the notion, put forward on several occasions in the story, that humans "were formed to be happy, and to contribute to the happiness of [their] fellow creatures" (194). The correspondents presented in this Canadian epistolary novel, moreover, seem less concerned than Pinckney with the tendency of love to fashion "the idol it worships" (220). In fact, one character in Brooke's novel unself-consciously confesses, with the author's approval, that his affection for his wife "is absolutely a species of idolatry" (181, cf. 201).

Given this mid-eighteenth-century Anglican context, it is noteworthy that Pinckney, like Brooke, cites secular authors far more often than the Bible and that her sparse biblical allusions are secularized (e.g., 15, 29, 53). These allusions, evidencing no sense of commentary tradition, do not emerge as occasions of logonomic conflict in her letter-book, and this absence may possibly suggest that such sites are more characteristic of Congregationalist, Presbyterian, and Quaker women. In any event, besides nurturing Pinckney's awareness of the expression of divine will in the world, Anglicanism also fostered her appreciation of personal identity, which her letters suggest was significant in comforting her.

To the north, neither Anne Bradstreet (c. 1612-72) in Massachusetts nor Esther Edwards Burr (1732-58) in New Jersey enjoyed quite the same comfort with the secular or with the female self. As a result, their personal struggle "not to fix [their] happiness on any thing beneath the supream Good nor Idolize the best man on Earth" resulted in deformations in their writings that intimate the underground existence of contesting sentiment.

Anne Bradstreet's Verse Letter to Her Husband

Anne Bradstreet, as observed in the introduction to my investigation, assures her readers and possibly herself that her writings are not intended as a challenge, as she puts it, to male "precedency" (McElrath and Robb 1981, 7) in the divinely ordained scheme of things, including the arts. Yet, as we also saw, she simultaneously insists in her "Prologue" that whatever may succeed in her verse should not be attributed to either chance or plagiarism. She accordingly instructs her readers to "grant some small acknowledgment" of her poetic capability (7).

The adjectival placement of the word "small" may be read to imply that such meager recognition is appropriate because the poet's accomplishment is minor, albeit nonetheless an accomplishment. But this reading exceeds the syntactic sense of Bradstreet's comment. She literally insists on the propriety of at least slight recognition of her achievement, an achievement that the textual placement of "small" does not necessarily qualify as minor. In fact, the issue of her actual poetic accomplishment is not addressed; it is evaded by

means of the strategic positioning of the word "small" before the word "acknowledgment."

This rhetorical maneuver may or may not be an instance of self-conscious irony. Bradstreet strikes some readers as proficient in the use of irony, especially in "The Prologue" (Eberwein 1981). Whether or not, in this particular instance, her placement of the word "small" represents conscious authorial intention unfortunately remains moot. Its narrative significance, on the other hand, is much less in question in light of its context: a verse prologue curiously reflecting the assertion and the gainsaying of poetic ingenuity. Here, as elsewhere in her work, bivocalness characterizes Bradstreet's attitude toward female creativity, a juggling of the opposite perspectives represented by the dual implications of the word "small."

Part of Bradstreet's problem, which also applied to her male peers, derived from the place of humility in Puritan theology. Humility was considered to be a radical virtue not readily compatible with the human production of art. The quest for such elusive humility is a main theme of Bradstreet's writings (Ball 1973). Nevertheless, beneath this conscious desire throughout her work, most especially in her elegies on infant deaths (Stanford 1974, 107-20; Mawer 1980), lie various buried clues that suggest an assertiveness bordering on resistance to authority. The rhythm of parts of her autobiography has likewise suggested to several readers (e.g., Wess 1976) that occasionally Bradstreet even experienced difficulty in honoring divine will.

Not everyone agrees, however, that such moments in Bradstreet's writing express genuine trouble with feelings of rebellion against divine and male authority or with feelings of insecurity over the assumption of the male role of authorship. Recently, these occasions have been read as artifice that either imitates the aesthetic conventions pertaining to humility (Margerum 1982) or follows the rhetorical conventions of self-examination, including the expression of one's confused thoughts as an endemic feature of everyone's struggle for salvation (Hammond 1993, 83-141). Such cautionary reconsiderations are noteworthy and deserve further study, especially in light of Bradstreet's extensive familiarity with various Renaissance and Reformed literary traditions.

Such readings identify substantial contextual elements of Bradstreet's literary heritage. Nevertheless, they also ignore others, such as the contemporary identification of writing with men and the related prevalent pattern, as generally expressed in the documents of sixteenth- and seventeenth-century women, of female discomfort in approaching this male activity (Waller 1974). Critics who stress Bradstreet's management of convention tend to imply, whether intentionally or not, that she could always consciously and fully convert her emotions into artifice, into a controlled rational or ironic discourse that perfectly contains her feelings. Within this undeclared assumption lurk unanswered questions about the likeliness of such a successful metamorphosis of emotion on every occasion and the naturalness of there being not even accidental signs of unruly resistance to the limits set on female identity and expression in Puritan culture. Even if, for the sake of argument, we were to accept the improbable proposition that such behavior is natural on both counts, we then must ponder what effect this confinement of Bradstreet's plaints to the artifice of convention—and surely we cannot restrict this confinement only to her expressions of self-deprecation—has on our ability to assess her meaning at any given point in her writings. If Bradstreet's meaning is masked by literary convention even in the later poems, moreover, then we also need to inquire further into the significance of her discontent with her highly conventional early verse after seeing it in print. Did her later verse, contrary to the recent claims made for it (Waller 1974; Laughlin 1970), *not* after all move toward greater independence and experiment in expression? I raise such queries less to refute the arguments for convention, which certainly have a claim to be considered, than to suggest that the issues these arguments are designed to address remain persistently complex. The arguments for convention, in other words, do not foreclose on or preempt all readings of actual, as opposed to archly contrived, tensions in Bradstreet's verse.

Such arguments particularly fail to account for the aesthetic dislocations in Bradstreet's verse. These moments are too peculiar to be construed entirely as the result of literary convention or tradition. Consider, for instance, the private and posthumously published poem "Upon the Burning of Our House, July 10th, 1666," in which a number of critics (e.g., Stanford 1966; Wess 1976; Martin 1979) have detected a tension between emotion and belief. This verse commences by recalling in detail many of the poet's prized material possessions lost in the fire. During most of the poem Bradstreet intently revisualizes these destroyed objects, only to stop the enumeration abruptly, as if some part of her mind has suddenly realized the impropriety of such a recollection. Indeed, before this brusque halt, the implicit direction of her poem threatens to unleash her anger at the deity, who ultimately is responsible for her loss. She halts this dangerous veering of her verse by interjecting, "Adeiu, Adeiu; All's Vanity" (McElrath and Robb 1981, 237).

The explicit sentiment of this line, safely ventriloquized in the language of Ecclesiastes 1:14, can readily be explained by arguments for the poet's application of literary and heuristic conventions. Turning to Scripture, as if to prayer, as a means of thwarting insurgent sentiment is culturally prescribed for a Puritan. What cannot be explained by these arguments is the aesthetic effect of this maneuver. To put the matter simply, something aesthetically disjunctive occurs in this short, stifled line when compared with what has preceded it in the poem. There is no "poetry" in this formulaic line, no detail, which is another way of saying that its alleged instruction does not inhabit the emotion-laden, well-furnished house of the poem as the poem has been constructed up to this point. The line is devoid of the harmony of aesthetics and emotion that has been evident until the appearance of this line.

Instead of reflecting the poetic embodiment of literary and rhetorical conventions—say, the decorum of imperfection (Mignon 1968) or the logogic site (Scheick 1992)—this particular line of verse records the sudden intrusion of an ideological convention from *outside* the aesthetic/domestic feelings, from *outside* the authorial presence, previously evident in the poem. As a site of logonomic conflict, the disruptive nature of this line may represent some theo-cratic ideal, but it also signals the flight of the poet from her poten-tially rebellious sentiment, as if the house of her emotion-full verse were also dangerously on fire.

The poem, in fact, now disintegrates into a "heap" of routine religious questions. These questions are "narratively" designed, with or without the poet's conscious consent, to suspend and contain the feelings featured in the first part of her poem. These conclud-ing questions reveal a bifurcating tension in the poet and her verse, whether or not she is aware of it. They indicate, finally, just how difficult it is for Bradstreet, at an unconscious level at least, to re-nounce her secularly valued material possessions and her secularly defined identity expressed in a smoldering anger over temporal losses.

"Upon My Son Samuel His Going to England, Novem. 6, 1657," another private and posthumously published verse, likewise con-veys "a hint of the struggle" between emotion and belief (White 1971, 309). It does so, narratively at least, by fissuring in a manner similar to "Upon the Burning of Our House." The later poem opens with Bradstreet's indication of the ways she will praise God if her son safely returns to her after his perilous transatlantic voyage. Af-ter sixteen well-managed lines of this sentiment, the poet abruptly interjects an extremely terse acknowledgment of an alternative pos-sibility: "If otherwise I goe to Rest, / Thy Will bee done, for that is best" (McElrath and Robb 1981, 228). Again the poet follows the Puritan cultural prescription to turn to Scripture, this time the Lord's Prayer (Luke 11:2), to counter unsanctioned sentiment. And again there is an aesthetic price paid as a result. The abbreviated and for-mulaic manner of these lines, akin to the sudden line of emotion-ally vacant formula in "Upon the Burning of Our House," intimates the flight of the poet from her poem, no longer a safe vessel of her emotion.

Cast adrift, the poet's abandoned feelings need mooring, and so in the next two concluding lines of her poem she asks the deity to "Perswade [her] heart" to accept divine will should this terrible event occur (228). The request for persuasion is also clearly an indication of her need to be persuaded. If the possible demise of her son is a thought Bradstreet must entertain, it is not a possibility that she can naturally accept, whatever the authority behind humility as the requisite response to mortality. Foundering on this discord, the poem (overfreighted with both disclosed and undisclosed feelings) can find no satisfying theocratic port. The poem is, accordingly, abandoned as the poet withdraws her emotional and aesthetic presence from the compromised vessel of her verse.

Such a performance in this poem and in "Upon the Burning of Our House," among many others, does not *successfully* conform to, or revise, or ironically engage any Renaissance literary tradition. If intended as hagiography in compliance with Reformed tradition, such a performance is likewise badly flawed because the idealized example of the second part is so pale, so flat, and so impoverished in aesthetic and emotional register when compared with the individualized fervid example of the first part. If my experience is typical, the more human first voice continues to linger, like an elegiac ghost, in the memory of the reader even after this voice has been hagiographically banished at the end of these two severely bifurcated poems.

The disruptive lines in "Upon the Burning of Our House" and "Upon My Son Samuel" indicate some deep conflict that cannot be perfectly negotiated by the application, revision, or ironic articulation of any literary convention or tradition available to the poet. The displacement of sentiment and aesthetics by arid formula results in the fracturing of both poems into two disjunctive pieces that the poet, much less the reader, cannot satisfactorily combine. Disclosure of feeling becomes nondisclosure, and this development signals the atrophication of both sentiment and artistry.

How much of this disjunction was perceived by the poet remains uncertain. Although both poems exist in manuscript only in her son Simon's hand, it is probably safe to assume that Bradstreet left them substantially as they are and so possibly did not quite see the effects of this conflict in her art. Today, for that matter, the rifts

beneath the surface of Bradstreet's art that result from the seismic
activity of constrained resistance and declared conformity are in-
visible to many readers. For our purposes, finally, two observations
are important: not everything in Bradstreet's verse can be identified as authorially deliberate, especially apropos tradition or convention; and occasionally her poems reveal unwittingly expressed
instances of logonomic conflict.

If Puritan theological insistence upon the virtue of humility contributed to the tension Bradstreet experienced between asserting and
restraining her voice, another problem for her was a cultural milieu
in which even a talented woman could not easily find authorization as a writer. Although in a long poem, written in 1643, that
departs from elegiac convention (Schweitzer 1988) Bradstreet presented Queen Elizabeth as a superb exemplar (Martin 1979) who
"hath wip'd off th' aspersion of her Sex, / That women wisdome
lack" (McElrath and Robb 1981, 156), she necessarily sought elsewhere for poetic embodiments of such wisdom. As indicated by a
review of the books with which Bradstreet was acquainted (Stanford
1974, 135-44), her models for authorship were evidently all men—
Virgil, Shakespeare, Spenser, Sidney, Raleigh, Foxe, Quarles, and
DuBartas, in particular. And her local audience was apparently primarily male—her father, her husband, her brother-in-law, among
others—who were encouraging, yet who at the same time could
not help but contribute to her anxiety as a female author lacking a
more universal authorization to write. The commendatory verse
prefacing her first appearance in *The Tenth Muse* (1650), however
well intentioned its male authors may have been, typically equivocated and condescended (Derounian-Stodola 1990). To be praised
for her exceptionality was also to be reminded of how much she
departed from (and potentially transgressed) cultural and universal
norms. Indeed, it is reasonable to surmise that Bradstreet anticipated a prevalent problem for earlier women writers, in general,
whenever they desired a sense of personal identity and at the same
sought recognition from male authority figures (Martin 1979).

At the start of her career, Bradstreet wrote poems that were largely imitative of male authors and traditions, and these writings least successfully recorded her own voice. After the publication of this early work in *The Tenth Muse,* Bradstreet's poetry underwent a change. In the later verse the poet, as if having looked into the mirror of her book and having found her work less worthy than she had hoped, became a more self-conscious writer more willing to engage personal matters in verse more varied in meter, structure, imagery, and subject matter. Some readers have understandably concluded that at this point Bradstreet discovered her voice (Laughlin 1970).

Closer study, however, suggests a more complex situation. Although in her later poems Bradstreet's presence is more personal and individualized, her voice still remains uncertain in the matter of its jurisdiction. In her later career the poet is less observant of male aesthetic traditions and is certainly *more* forthright in the expression of her emotions, but she also continues to ground her self-expression in the male-determined interpretations of Scripture. If Bradstreet's later writings rely particularly on scriptural typology (Rosenmeier 1977), this ministerial manner, it needs also to be observed, becomes a site of anxiety apparently beyond the poet's awareness. Illustrative of this situation is "A Letter to Her Husband, Absent upon Publick Employment," inserted posthumously in the second edition of her verse, *Several Poems* (1678):

> My head, my heart, mine Eyes, my life, nay more,
> My joy, my Magazine of earthly store,
> If two be one, as surely thou and I,
> How stayest thou there, whilst I at Ipswich lye?
> So many steps, head from the heart to sever
> If but a neck, soon should we be together:
> I like the earth this season, mourn in black,
> My Sun is gone so far in's Zodiack,
> Whom whilst I 'joy'd, nor storms, nor frosts I felt,
> His warmth such frigid colds did cause to melt.
> My chilled limbs now nummed lye forlorn;
> Return, return sweet Sol from Capricorn;
> In this dead time, alas, what can I more

Then view those fruits which through thy heat I bore?
Which sweet contentment yield me for a space,
True living Pictures of their Fathers face.
O strange effect! now thou art Southward gone,
I weary grow, the tedious day so long;
But when thou Northward to me shalt return,
I wish my Sun may never set, but burn
Within the Cancer of my glowing breast,
This welcome house of him my dearest guest.
Where ever, ever stay, and go not thence,
Till natures sad decree shall call thee hence;
Flesh of thy flesh, bone of thy bone,
I here, thou there, yet both but one. (181)

This verse letter features the zodiac as a source for metaphors to describe the poet's wintry state of mind as a result of the distance of her sunlike husband, away from Ipswich on business. She anticipates his return, like "sweet Sol from Capricorn," to "burn / Within the Cancer of [her] glowing breast." Bradstreet sustains this analogy, including an intimation of sexual congress when referring to her children as "those fruits which through [his] heat [she] bore." Derived from the sort of information that was readily available in almanacs, this analogy primarily maintains a secular identity in her poem until the concluding lines, which allude to Scripture: "Flesh of thy flesh, bone of thy bone, / I here, thou there, yet both but one."

The appearance of the corporeal images of bone and flesh at the end of the poem has been prepared for by preceding references to head, face, eyes, neck, breast, heart, limbs, and sexual congress. This body motif coalesces with the zodiac motif when, for instance, the poet indicates that the wintry state associated by the withdrawal of her sunlike husband potentially threatens her life: "My chilled limbs now nummed lye forlorn." It is important to observe, nevertheless, that both motifs are secular as used in this poem and that as a narrative field they do not *inherently* prepare for the sudden attempted displacement or translation of their secular province into the official biblical context contained in the last two lines of the poem.

The last two lines of Bradstreet's verse letter echo Adam's response to the deity's creation of Eve from his rib (Schweitzer 1991, 177). The Geneva version reads:

Then the man [Adam] said, This is bone of my bones, and flesh of my flesh. She shal be called woman, because she was taken out of man.

Therefore shal man leaue his father and his mother, and shal cleave to his wife, and they shal be one flesh. [Gen. 2:23-24]

These Old Testament verses are repeated by Jesus, as the Second Adam (Matt. 19:5), and later by Saint Paul, apropos the relationship between Christ and the church:

we are members of his [the Lord's] body, of his flesh, and of his bones.

For this cause shall a man leave father and mother, and shall cleave to his wife, and they twaine shall be one flesh.

This is a great secret, but I speak concerning Christ, and concerning the Church. [Eph. 5:30-32]

Routinely associating these Old and New Testament passages, biblical commentaries of Bradstreet's time instruct that these passages refer to the silent subordination of the second sex to men, the reverence wives owe to their husbands, and the literal and typological nobility of wedlock. The Pauline passage, moreover, is said to refer to the mystical marriage of the church, as bride, and the Savior, as bridegroom.

Consequently, in response to my observation that Bradstreet's poem does not internally provide for the transition from terrestrial narrative field to biblical province, one might object that Puritan culture routinely encouraged analogies between the secular and the divine, especially between physical marriage and spiritual conversion (Daly 1978, 6-39). During the seventeenth century, in fact, marriage imagery was pervasive in Anglo-American sermonic discourse (Morgan 1966, 161-68). Although this imagery would disappear during the following century as a result of post-Reformation changes in ministerial thought (Winship 1992), previously and frequently the marriage motif served in sermons as a reminder of the union of the elect with the Christic spouse, as Bradstreet likewise makes clear in her late manuscript poem, "As a Weary Pilgrim." Bradstreet's biblical contextualization of her physical attraction to her husband, it therefore might be plausibly argued, "is entirely orthodox" (Porterfield, *Spirituality,* 1992, 110) and indicates "comfort" in her "subordinate position" in "a union that . . . foreshadows the eternal union" with Christ (Schweitzer 1991, 177).

Such judgments must be conceded, especially if we are principally seeking Bradstreet's conscious determination in her work. And were such judgments applied to, say, "In My Solitary Hours in My Dear Husband His Absence" (extant in Simon's hand), there would be perhaps little more to say. For in this fearful, if nonetheless diplomatic, poem Bradstreet indeed seems to try to derive genuine comfort from the correlation of earthly and divine unions:

> Tho: husband dear bee from me gone
> Whom I doe loue so well
> I haue a more beloued one
> Whose comforts far excell.
> [McElrath and Robb 1981, 234]

In this contemplative verse-prayer the orthodox subordination of human marriage to Christic union is clearly part of the theocratic transaction of the poem, from its beginning to its end.

In contrast, a similar theocratic transaction (of some kind, at least) emerges with equal clarity only at the end of "A Letter to Her Husband." To read this transaction backward into the poem, so as to claim its presence throughout, is to seize upon possible nuances from the margin of the two main complexes of imagery (the body and the zodiac). A nuance, for example, might be detected when the poet designates the husband as the head of the wife, which may be a muted echo of Ephesians 5:23. Another nuance might be detected in the poet's anticipation of a personal springlike revival following the return of her sunlike husband ("dearest guest"), which may be seen as typifying the reception of saving grace during earthly

life, the Second Coming of Christ, or the beatific vision of the redeemed after death. Such readings are certainly enabled by the Puritan association of earthly signs and spiritual referents.

But if they are thusly theocratically enabled, they are at the same
time *narratively* disabled in the poem. The issue of whether or not
such moments are intended biblical nuances aside, they all occur at
the fringe of the main field of interest, imagery, and drama of the
poem. This peripheral position in the narrative field raises important questions. If "A Letter to Her Husband" is indeed about marriage as a foreshadowing of eternal union with Christ, should it
not then directly and firmly point in that direction, as is required
by the divine audience of the diplomatic "In My Solitary Hours"?
The peripheral position of possible biblical allusions makes their
presence appear more latent than actualized.

Moreover, their reduction to latency and marginality facilitates
their apparent narrative function as a means rather than an end.
They seem, in other words, to reverse the standard movement from
type (means) to antitype (end). Narratively, their antitypical value
(the design of the typological system) appears to be transformed
into a means of authorizing the type—in this specific instance, the
otherwise potentially dangerous intensity of the physical bond between Simon and Anne.

In fact, the sudden emergence of biblical context at the end of
Bradstreet's poem oddly casts more of a backward shadow than a
backward light on the prominent zodiac and body imagery. In effect, the abrupt surfacing of religious context accidentally empha-
sizes the pronounced absence of a similarly *explicit* religious context
in the preceding lines. Such imagery of the body and the zodiac
has a long tradition of Christianization (see Edward Taylor's "Meditation 1.19" [Stanford 1960], for example), but in Bradstreet's poem
this tradition is at best latent until the end, when it is *possibly* activated. If it is activated at that point, the biblical allusions in the last
two lines of her poem make all the more obvious that the typing of
the bridegroom of the soul through the imagery of sun and head
should have been clear from the first. Yet it is not. This analogical

function is at best, if at all, dutifully tacked on at the end, where it possibly serves to legitimate what has gone before by placing it safely within a theocratic context and where at the same time it potentially serves to intimate improperly the separate identity of this very same secular forematter.

Such a narrative performance supports the pertinent critical observation that "the ardor with which Bradstreet addresses her husband . . . threatens to overshadow a proper love of God by placing so high a value on one who is a mere creature" (Stanford 1974, 26). This threat is fairly substantial, viewed in terms of narrative performance, despite the possibility that eventually the poet may theocratically contextualize her earthly affection as an adumbration of divine union. In effect, her intensity of focus on Simon, earthly marriage, and the poet herself inadvertently invites prohibited graven images (Lev. 26:1) to appear on the horizon of the verse love letter. In her children, for example, she sees "living pictures of their [absent] father's face"; that is to say, she sees the image of Simon in them, not the image of God.

In repeating Adam's words, furthermore, she to some extent appropriates an Adamic identity, however unknowingly. And not only do these words—"Flesh of thy flesh, bone of thy bone"—point to traditional scriptural commentary on the subjection and reverence that wives owe to their husbands, but also these same words in some sense convey the author's self-worship in the act of adoring her husband, with whom she claims to be one. Saint Paul opened the door to this possibility—albeit it was evidently not at all what he had in mind—in the same passages we have been considering: "He that loveth his wife loveth himselfe" (Eph. 5:28). So also, in the Adamic/Pauline terms inserted at the end of Bradstreet's poem, she who loves her husband and the image of her husband reflected in their children likewise loves herself.

And by alluding in the final line of her poem to Saint Paul's commentary on Jesus' repetition of Adam's words about marriage, "I here, thou there, yet both but one," Bradstreet appears to bracket, at least unconsciously, Saint Paul's specific reminder of its ultimate application to Christ's marriage to the church. This mystical meaning, so obvious from the outset in "In My Solitary Hours," is conspicuously absent in "A Letter to Her Husband." The poet cites only half of the authorization provided by Saint Paul and *in effect* stresses the lesser of the two meanings of Saint Paul's comment. To some degree this emphasis covertly reinstates the poet's secular sentiment, as if it could stand alone (even though Saint Paul says it cannot) without its higher allegorical meaning. This tendency not only reverses the customary direction from type to antitype but also rears up the poet's marriage to Simon as another potential graven image.

To make these observations is not to suggest that Bradstreet was, wittingly or unwittingly, guilty of idolatry. It is to suggest that whatever her intentions might have been, the narrative of her poem reveals certain contrary tendencies or veerings responsive to undeclared or unrecognized desires. It is to say that if for the sake of argument we admit claims for the poet's deliberate and unironic effort to accommodate ideology through typology in "A Letter to Her Husband," we are still left with the problem of the peculiarities of the poem's narrative performance, including peripheral nuances that are not quantitatively or qualitatively superior to, or equal to, the secular province of the poem. This narrative outcome conflicts with the theocratic ideal, which positions antitypical matter above typical matter. Nor can this conflict be resolved by suggesting that the intrusive scriptural allusion at the end of the poem activates the nuances and releases them from their latency at the edge of the verse letter. Such an intrusion, not to mention its overt biblical language, draws special attention to itself, in part by suggesting its divergence from what has gone before. This intrusiveness, departure, and alteration in language collectively imply a sense of correction, revision, or reorientation of the previous matter of the poem. In their narrative performance, they intimate division, rather than typological harmony, between the parts of the verse letter.

In other words, whether or not the culminating biblical allusion participates in a debatable attempt to centralize what has been peripheral and to marginalize what has been central, it tellingly compromises the poem as narrative. The manner in which the poem bifurcates, dividing between twenty-four lines of authorial engagement with her zodiac/body analogies and two closing lines of authorial self-erasure, intimates some underground pressure producing distortions in the narrative surface of the verse letter. This effect was probably beyond the author's recognition. In any event, experienced as narrative, her poem does not overtly integrate the secular and the divine from the outset. Only at the end, and very abruptly, does the poet require a scriptural authorization for what has gone before in her love letter, in which the secular not only predominates but also engages the poet's feelings much more intensely than is registered in her abdication of voice and identity in the allusive final lines.

Just what scriptural authorization she had in mind is a query far more difficult to answer than generally has been perceived. There is, in short, still another problem in attempting to use the scriptural allusion at the end of Bradstreet's poem to centralize what has hypothetically been typologically latent and marginal. To find, in retrospect, typological implications in the verse letter on the basis of its last lines is to assume without question that these lines allude to Ephesians 5:30-32 and not to Genesis 2:23-24. Although Protestant biblical commentaries relate these two passages, they make a distinction that is important apropos Bradstreet's poem. The Genesis passage expresses the deity's sanctification of marriage as honorable in itself, whereas the Ephesians passage expresses the mystical (antitypical) meaning of marriage. It is impossible to know for certain which passage authorizes the sentiment of Bradstreet's love letter. Both could do so, but in very different ways. It is interesting to note, however, that in contrast to the standard Pauline explanation of the verses from Ephesians, the orthodox interpretation of the verses from Genesis seems, in quantitative terms, more suitable to both the centrality of the secular imagery and the marginality of possible biblical nuance in Bradstreet's poem.

No matter which of the two different possibilities one arbitrarily assigns to Bradstreet's openly displayed (if referentially uncertain) scriptural allusion, the shift from the secular to the religious arena as the final focus of her verse letter amounts, in narrational terms, to a distortion of the poem. Symmetry has been violated, quite possibly against the grain of the poet's motivating desire behind the undertaking of this work. And it is precisely at this logonomic site of conflict between regulating sets of rules (the personal and the theocratic) that we glimpse the poet's unintended crisis over authority, here expressed in an anxious need to renegotiate what she has written.

This narrative pattern certainly vexes the radical assertion that Bradstreet's verse "celebrates a sexual union that resonates with the divine" because the poet "believed the body to be filled with the presence of Christ" and discerned "the hidden Christ, both in the workings of nature and in the human body" (Rosenmeier 1991, 116-17, 125). This is an extreme and improbable reading of a Congregationalist poet whose writings do not anywhere explicitly reveal such an heretical posture. Indeed, such a view would have shocked Bradstreet and her immediate contemporaries, those astute students of Origen and other church fathers who specifically refuted such notions of Christian gnosticism.

It is true that the Augustinian heritage of the Puritans provided for a certain valuation of the material world, including the human body, because it posited no real gap between the order of nature and the order of grace (Scheick 1974, 27-48). The human body, for example, was created good from the first, was redemptively assumed by the Son of God, and would be reunited with the elect souls in heaven. Even in its most pristine mode, however, the body was (in Augustinian terms) created ex nihilo, like the rest of the natural order, and therefore was distinctly separate in its being, even if related by the Spirit to the divine order. Moreover, if the body's inherent goodness remained untainted, this essential quality was latent only in postlapsarian humanity. For the Puritans, the temporal body—as opposed to the prelapsarian, the Christic, or the resurrected body—was (in Pauline terms) the *flesh,* the body in a corrupt state prone to misdirection and rebellion.

This is one of the points made in Bradstreet's "The Flesh and the Spirit," a poem in which the corrupt body can only ask insolent questions of its twin sister, the soul, because it is as yet still the "unregenerate part" in need of rescue from postlapsarian "shadows" and "fancies vain." The harmonious interaction between these "two sisters"—the always latent harmony between the order of nature and the order of grace—will once again be made manifest after the Last Judgment; until then (when the body has been "laid in th' dust") there is, as spirit says to flesh, a "deadly feud 'twixt thee and me" (McElrath and Robb 1981, 175-77). The subject matter of "The Flesh and the Spirit" is utterly conventional, which is my very point: Bradstreet was not a Christian Gnostic who viewed the corrupt human body, the temporal manifestation of the human body, as a vessel suffused with Christ. It had not been such a vessel even in its most pristine mode, and this separateness accounts in part for Bradstreet's inability to integrate successfully the secular and the divine in "A Letter to Her Husband," which emotionally and narratively countenances the secular far beyond its theocratically authorized function as a sign of a divine referent.

It was not likely to have been otherwise, at least for Bradstreet as we have come to know her through her writings. Just how natural such a tendency would be for her can be gauged by two indicative moments elsewhere. One is an admonition appearing in Martha Brewster's post-1740 verse letter to her sister-in-law. Martha warns Huldah Brewster, on the eve of her marriage to John Goold: "Yet bear in Mind, tho' Love be Kind, / Least too much love of Goold, / Provoke the Lord, your Soul Defraud" (Brewster 1758, 30). Another and earlier instance emerges in a confession of conflict in Mehitulde Parkman's 1683 letter to her husband. "Ms Mechison tells me often she fears that I love you more than god," Mehitulde reports. Here she tells her husband something unsayable except in a virtual code and reveals to us just how much trouble some Puri-

tan women had, consciously or unconsciously, in truly subordinat-
ing and conforming emotional human attachments to a system of
belief that insisted on assessing such attachments only as dehuman-
izing images and shadows of the divine. Mehitulde, like Bradstreet,
concludes her statement by seeking the safety of scriptural allusion
(Matt. 10:37); she writes, "he that loves father or mother more than
me is not worthee of me" (Ulrich 1982, 109). This is a poignant
move, if we sense the author's desperation over the witchery of desire and feeling that the authorized biblical allusion is meant to re-
prove and exorcise.

Like Bradstreet's elegy on the burning of her home, her paean to
her husband had to be reined, its secular sentiment licensed only
by its subordination to religious definition, as required by the Augustinian tradition so ingrained in the Puritan *mentalité*. In some
part of her mind, as she wrote this verse letter to her husband,
Bradstreet apparently sensed—I suggest no more than *sensed*—the
need for a proper contextualization for her celebration of physical
love. Reformed biblical commentaries and Puritan sermonic practice provided the ready analogy for this suitable contextualization,
but in this instance—whether indeed Ephesians or Genesis was the
source of her allusion—this analogy could not resolve the conflict
between the poet's internally authorized feeling and her equally sin-
cere externally authorized belief.

In short, the identifying signature of Anne Bradstreet's sentiment
is found in the ongoing logonomic conflict reflected in the final
move of her verse letter. At this site of conflict between regulating
sets of rules (the personal and the theocratic) the harmonious union
of sentiment and aesthetics is "put asunder" (Matt. 19:6), scape-
goated on behalf of the nearly idolatrous intensity of her feelings
about her marriage. At this site we can glimpse the poet's inadvert-
ent crisis over authority, here expressed in an anxious renegotiation
of what she has written. On the one hand, she seems to retreat from
the poem and to silence her own voice—the voice that had invested
so much of itself in the secular part (all but two lines) of the poem.
This voice represses its personal identity by impersonally ventrilo-

quizing biblical allusions that serve the same watchman function as the one in Mehitulde Parkman's letter to her husband. On the other hand, this presumably voluntary act of renunciation conveys more than a sign of mere conformity to orthodoxy and comfort in submission. The narrative implications of this move resist and confute the poet's likely self-conscious renunciation by drawing special attention to what she retreats from and what she silences.

As we have seen, this narrative performance includes the sudden intrusion of openly declared biblical allusions that attempt to displace the poet's voice and identity; the unstable relationship of this intrusion between the apparent centrality of intense secular experience and the possible latency or marginality of divine signification in the verse letter; the allied potential narrative inversion of typological discourse, with the antitype serving as a means rather than an end in the authorization of physical love; the similarly allied tendency to idolize Simon, marriage, and the author by means of both narrative focus and referentially unclear biblical allusions; and the fragmenting of the verse letter into two unequal parts, not only quantitatively but also qualitatively, with each segment evidencing a distinct and different emotional register. Although Bradstreet chooses renunciation and attempts the erasure of authorial presence, the narrative drama of her poem insistently, resistantly writes her signature large.

Esther Edwards Burr's Letter-Journal

"When Mr Burr is gone," Esther Edwards Burr confesses to her confidante Sarah Prince (1728-71), the recipient of the letters in Burr's journal, "I am ready to immagine the sun does not give so much light as it did, when my best self was at home, and I am in the glooms two [too], half de[a]d, my Head gone. Behead a person and they will soon die" (Karlsen and Crumpacker 1984, 81). Although written a little more than a century later, the imagery used by the daughter of Jonathan Edwards concerning the absence of her husband (Aaron) is identical to Anne Bradstreet's in "A Letter to Her Husband." As we noted in the Introduction, Burr likewise shares Bradstreet's experience of the taboo status of writing as a cultural pursuit for women and as an expression of female identity. Also like Bradstreet, Esther Edwards Burr unconsciously registers at the emotional center of her narrative performance a potentially transgressive valuation of the material image of God in human relationships.

The most significant difference between Burr and Bradstreet, at least concerning their expression of spousal sentiments, is perhaps unexpected, especially since the narrative space of the epistolary medium during the colonial period is less bound by moral (male) authority (Kenyon 1992, xix) than is the verse medium. Burr at mid-eighteenth century seems *in some respects* more conservative than Bradstreet at mid-seventeenth century. This feature may not be immediately evident because with the exception of citing the bases of sermons she has heard, Burr alludes to Scripture infrequently in her correspondence. Her manner may disguise the fact that whereas Bradstreet is able (however problematically) to contextualize biblically her celebration of physical love, Burr appears unable to do so. As an eighteenth-century Presbyterian, Burr cannot access the Renaissance appreciation of life that Bradstreet inherits and coalesces with her Reformed response to the world; nor, on the other hand, is Burr able to benefit from the Deistic celebration of human potentiality in the world that she has manifestly encountered in her reading. Burr sees her attachment to the quotidian, including her intense affection for her husband, as utterly without any approved authorization. So the unacknowledged strategy of abrupt displacement through scriptural legitimation evident at the end of Bradstreet's "A Letter to Her Husband" dwindles to the unacknowledged strategy of displacement through denial in Burr's letter home concerning the demise of her husband. In lieu of Bradstreet's Renaissance heritage, Burr inherits the minimalist version of Puritanism promoted by her reactionary father, Jonathan Edwards. This inheritance includes an eschatological obliteration of all temporal images and shadows of the divine (Scheick 1992, 69-119).

Esther Edwards Burr's legacy informs her self-castigation concerning spiritual "deadness" (Karlsen and Crumpacker 1984, 61),
a characteristic feature of her epistolary journal: "I wish I could be
willing to be and do, and suffer, just what God pleased without
any will of my own, but I am stubborn, willfull, disobedient. . . .
How unfit am I to ap[p]roach the Lords Table" (131). Even the
Lord's Supper, approached in Presbyterian expectation rather than
Congregationalist restraint, does not help her: "I hoped to have meet
[met] My Lord and Savior at his Table. But to my grief find no
great alteration"; "I was in great hoopes [hopes] of meeting Christ
in some extreordinary manner at his Table, but alas God has
dissappointed me!" (78, 131). Acknowledging "how apt be we to
set our hearts on the injoyments of time and sense," Burr laments,
"My heart, I see is on the World and not on God!" (68, 84).

In particular her heart is set on two people. One is Sarah Prince,
the daughter of the Boston minister Thomas Prince. The intensity of
Esther's affection for Sarah can be gauged in a letter of 1755: "How
over joyed I have just now been! I could not help weeping for joy
to hear once more from my dear, very dear Fidelia [Sarah]. . . . I
broke it open with [as] much e[a]gerness as ever a fond lover
imbraced the dearest joy and d[e]light of his soul" (97). Assessed in
the context of the journal as a whole, the intensity of emotion here
is genuine, not a matter of convention. The analogy to the lover,
with the unrecognized, significant displacement of what in Puritan
terms ought to be the true joy and delight of a *soul*, illuminates for
us a crucial feature of Burr's indictment of herself as "carnel, fleshly,
Worldly minded, and Devilish" (127).

Indeed, it is likewise as a lover that her heart is set upon her
husband, whose absences invariably make her feel benighted, be-
headed, and dying. If the communion with the Son in the Lord's
Supper is unable to reverse Esther's feeling of spiritual deadness,
communion with her sunlike Aaron reinvigorates her life: "I re-
ceived a very affectionate Letter from Mr Burr, which did me more
good than ever a Cordial did when I was faint. I was before extreamly
low-spirited, but at once I felt as lively as ever I did in my life"

(55). Time and again, "so lonely" that "every minute seems an hour" (46, 101), she anticipates Aaron's return with a fervor that in contrary Edwardsean moments she knows ought to be decarnalized and directed toward Christ. No wonder, then, that she is "affraid" she might "provoke God," her soul's bridegroom, "by set[t]ing [her] heart two [too] much on this dear gentleman, to take him from" her: "and—Alas what would all the world be to me if he were out of it!" (106).

So intense are her feelings on this occasion that she does not focus on the appropriateness of such a loss of attachment to the world, which is the authorized response she elsewhere observes when contemplating the disheartening French defeat of General Edward Braddock near Fort Duquesne: "that it might teach us to depend whol[l]y on God, and not on an Arm of flesh!" (137). In contrast, during her husband's nearly fatal illness, she confesses: "I cant be resighned to the Will of God if it is to bereave me of all that is near and dear at one stroke! I can see it [as] infinitely just, but I [c]ant be willing that justice should take place . . . O pray for that I may have a right temper of mind towards the ever blessed God!" (146-47).

Did she attain this ideal state of mind when Aaron Burr died on 24 September 1757, two years after this candid revelation? Her journal of intimate letters to Sarah ends three weeks before his demise, and the subsequent, certainly guarded correspondence to her parents is difficult to assess in this regard. In her letters home, usually addressed to her mother but always read by both parents, Esther reports on 7 October 1757, "I think I have been enabled to cast my care upon him [God], and have found great peace and calmness in my mind" (293).

Her hesitant "I think" may possibly raise a doubt in our mind, particularly when at the end of her letter Esther entreats her parents "to request earnestly of the Lord, that I may never despise his chastenings, nor faint under this his severe stroke; of which I am sensible there is great danger, if God should only deny me the supports that he has hitherto graciously granted" (294). Given what we know of Esther Burr's feelings, as expressed in her much less guarded letters to Sarah Prince, we might become especially sensitive to her fear of being in "great danger." Her parents, and probably Esther herself, may have read in this expression a fear of some kind of rebellion against God, such as despair and even suicide. But, as we will see, these possible future transgressions overlay a prior, unacknowledged offense.

A month later (2 November 1757) she reassures her father that she has accepted divine will. Now further stressed by the near death of one of her children, she thinks of "the glorious state [her] dear departed Husband must be in" and then her "soul [is] carried out in such longing desires after this glorious state" (296). Was it the state of glory that her fatigued spirit desired, or was it reunion with her husband, about whom she had once speculated, "What would all the world be to me if he were out of it"?

Burr's allusion to Job 13:15 in the same letter—"[God] enabled me to say that altho' thou slay me yet will I trust in thee" (295)— may seem to answer our question if we overlook what it displaces. Such contemporary commentaries as Matthew Henry's specify, apropos this passage from Job, that we must have faith in God *as a friend* even if He afflicts us as an enemy. This allusion, with its embedded subject of friendship, functions as a site of logonomic conflict in Esther's letter; it unsurely negotiates the authorized theological ideal of divine relationship represented in the official Reformed commentaries on Job and the unauthorized emotional value of human relationship represented in the intimate letters by Burr.

"Nothing is more refreshing to the soul (except communication with God himself) then [than] the company and society of a friend," Esther Burr tells Sarah Prince in 1756; "One that has the spirit off [of], and relish for, true friendship—this is becoming [to] the rational soul—this is God-like," "'Tis the Life of Life" (185). A year earlier she had spoken similarly: "To tell the truth when I speak of the world, and the things that are in the World, I dont mean friends, for friendship does not belong to the world. True friendship is first inkindled by a spark from Heaven, and heaven will never suffer it to go out, but it will burn to all Eternity" (92). This deep sentiment is informed in part by a contemporary female regard for the special bond between women (Pettengill 1992), the sort of regard evident two years later in Martha Wadsworth Brewster's advice to her daughter: "Esteem a real Friend, if such there be" (Brewster 1758, 34). Such sentiment concerning human relationships characterizes Esther's attachment to Sarah, whose missives she reads "with [as] much e[a]gerness as ever a fond lover imbraced the dearest joy and d[e]light of his soul" (97); and it informs her attachment to Aaron, whom she would not exchange "for any person, or thing, or all things on E[a]rth. . . . Not for a Million such Worlds as this that had no Mr Burr in it" (92).

Esther properly gave priority to "communication with God himself." Had she lived to read Phillis Wheatley's "Hymn to Humanity" (1773), Esther would have concurred that Christ alone extends "Immortal Friendship" (Mason 1989, 96). Esther indeed knew well her father's doctrinal insistence upon an ecstatic, atemporal, spiritual sense of the heart as the only possible sign of this divine communication. She had in fact experienced his attitude firsthand, such as the occasion when she was close to death and he was less concerned with fostering her recovery than with exhorting her at this time "to lot upon [count on] no Happiness here" (286). Moreover, she was doubtless far more sensitive to her beloved mother's personal experience of this spiritual sense of the heart when Esther was a child. Always much closer to her mother than to her father, Esther likely measured her own spiritual condition against the model of Sarah Pierpont Edwards, especially as presented in Jonathan's *Some Thoughts Concerning the Present Revival of Religion in New-England* (1742).

In presenting this account, her father had altered his wife's version of her religious experience, making it reflect an abstract inner purity of motive utterly indifferent to social context (Ellison 1984). He reported a state of soul "wherein the whole world, with the dearest enjoyments in it, were renounced . . . [and] seemed perfectly to

vanish into nothing" (Goen 1972, 333). Edwards particularly speci-
fied Sarah's exemplary "resignation of the lives of dearest earthly
friends . . . having [instead] nothing but God"—"as it were seeing
him, and sensibly immediately conversing with him" as one's sole/
soul intimate (340).

Esther may consciously subordinate human friendship to "communication with God himself," yet it is precisely this doctrinally
imposed superior friendship, the Edwardsean new sense of the heart,
that is missing from the "soul" of both her intimate correspondence
with Sarah Prince and her intimate remarks about Aaron Burr. These
letters not only overtly attest to the spiritual "deadness" of a "heart
[set] . . . on the World and not on God"; they also covertly under-
cut their obligatory concession to the primacy of divine friendship.
The concession is overwhelmed by the sheer power of the true emotional center of the letters, a reservoir of dramatically expressed feeling similar to that in Bradstreet's "A Letter to Her Husband." Such
emotion indeed "tell[s] the truth"—that, in effect, Esther's love for
Aaron and Sarah has been "more refreshing to [her] soul," has been
more the "Life of [her] Life," than has "communication with [the]
God" who "dissappoint[s]" her desire for religious affections even
in the sacrament of the Lord's Supper. Human friendship, "inkindled
by a spark from Heaven," is divine for Esther. It "does not belong
to the world," but it is indeed found *in* the world; and it is found
there for Esther far more efficaciously than is divine friendship per
se. Her record of this efficacy, the experiential heart of her affection for Sarah and Aaron, *narratively* values "God-like" human relationships over God, the image of the divine over divinity.

In other words, against her conscious aim and *at the level of feeling,* Esther inadvertently prizes the image of God (Aaron and Sarah) more than God. Similar to the implication in Bradstreet's poem,
the emotional force of Esther's inner life—positioning strong physical affection for a divine "likeness," for a graven image, over weak
spiritual affection for God—veers toward a violation of the second
commandment: "Thou shalt have no other gods before me" (Ex.
20:3). This "carnel, fleshly, Worldly minded, and Devilish" *idoliza-*

tion of "the Life of Life" is the unacknowledged "great danger" intimated in Esther's allusion to Job. Expressed in a "public" letter to her watchman-like parents rather than in a "private" letter to Sarah Prince, this ventriloquized allusion represents two competing sites of authority: the official Edwardsean version of friendship based on an abstract ideal and the outlawed Estherean version of friendship based on an intense emotion. As a shrouded site of logonomic conflict, this allusion to Job explicitly, officially declares faith in divine friendship as supreme and at the same time implicitly, secretly, and elegiacally recalls Esther's transgressive valuation of human friendship as supreme.

This double sense likewise inheres in Burr's proclamation that human friendship "will burn to all Eternity." The nuances in this instance include more than the suggestion of a reunion of loved ones in heaven (certainly one aspect of Esther's "longing desires after this glorious state" following Aaron's death); they also suggest a concealed fantasy in which the secular displaces or at least parallels the divine. Esther's desire for an eternal reunion with her intimate friends seems to transcend her desire for the beatific vision—hardly a pattern of thought supported by the concept of eternal love held by her father.

Sarah Prince's eulogy, entered in her private notebook on 21 April 1758, provides a further glimpse into the nature of the conflict over authority lodged in her friend's attitude toward human relationships. Prince heads this tribute to her dead friend with an apt cautionary note: "GOD will have no Rival in the heart which he sanctifies for himself" (Karlsen and Crumpacker 1984, 307). The threat of idolatry, as we noted, is the "great danger" lurking just below the surface of Esther's awareness; and it is the peril that Sarah tries to keep as steadily in mind as did Mehitulde Parkman. Mourning the death of Esther, "the Apple of [her] Eye," and remembering "the Lovely Pattern she set," Sarah laments, "She was mine! O the tenderness which tied our hearts!" (307). Now her "Earthly joy is gone!" Now, too, her "God hides his Face!" She "can't see Love in this dispensation!" (308). She resolves, nevertheless, "to live loose from the World . . . and have done with Idols" (308).

The words "have done with Idols" indicate Sarah's retrospective suspicion that her relationship with Esther may have verged on the idolatrous. The demise of her life "Pattern" has exposed the danger of a relationship that potentially rivals God in the human heart. Whereas Eliza Pinckney warns against "Idoliz[ing] the best man on Earth," Sarah Prince admonishes herself against the idolization of a female model of "Natural Powers . . . superior to most Women" (307).

The trajectory of the increasing idolization of a loved one that we have chronologically traced from Anne Bradstreet's verse concerning her absent husband to Esther Burr's letter concerning her deceased husband and Sarah Prince's eulogy concerning her departed friend reaches an apogee in Annis Boudinot Stockton's poem concerning her absent husband. The well-educated daughter of wealthy French Huguenot (Calvinist) immigrants who settled in Philadelphia and later in the Princeton area of New Jersey, Annis enjoyed an elite social status, married well, and attended to societal and political affairs far more than to religious matters. Her interests were primarily secular, and when she infrequently turned her attention to religious issues, the neoclassical results register a relatively low level of personal emotion. In fact, religious imagery and biblical allusions in Stockton's writings principally serve secular ends and evince no discernible signs of the kind of tensions we have seen in the writings of Bradstreet, Burr, and Prince.

"Epistle—To Lucius" (c. 1766), written while Annis Stockton's husband Richard ("Lucius") was abroad on business, provides an especially interesting example in light of its nominal affinity to Anne Bradstreet's "A Letter to Her Husband, Absent upon Publick Employment." In her poem Stockton appropriates religious language and references to embellish her declaration of spousal love. She speaks, accordingly, of her uxorial admiration as akin both to the amazement of "Sheba's queen" in Solomon's court (1 Kings 10) and to "A votaries prayer"; she likewise speaks of her husband's "sweet voice with fascinating grace" and of how the "lov'd Idea [of him] would engross [her] mind" (Mulford 1995, 89). Her poem concludes, moreover, with fervid imagery suggesting an ecstatic intertwining of light and flesh: "may wit and elegance bestow / Some emanation bright some softer glow / Some sweet at[t]ractive that thy heart may twine / (Stronger than beauty) with each nerve of mine" (89). Such a moment recalls the language of religious mystics, but here as in the other cited passages religious nuances (Sheba, prayer, grace, engrossing love, bright emanation, and sweet attraction) surrender their charge of spiritual significance to the poet's celebration of her earthly affection. The religious undercurrent of these nuances is stilled and so does not tug against Stockton's express intention. The only anxiety evident in her poem is the one she conventionally confesses concerning her ability to please her husband: "Oh Could my anxious heart but once believe" that "I have the power to please," for "so conscious of my own demerit / In contemplating thee I lose my spirit."

In contrast to Annis Stockton's thoroughly secularized sentiment here, contemplation for Anne Bradstreet, Esther Burr, and Sarah Prince is ideally an opportunity to invigorate, rather than lose, one's spirit. Of course, for Bradstreet, Burr, and Prince the word "spirit," especially when appearing in conjunction with the word "contemplating," primarily refers to religious concerns and only secondarily to temporal concerns. As we have seen, the underground challenge to this very hierarchy, as fostered by deeply entrenched emotions resistant to authority at some critical point, imparts a special drama to their writings. Such logonomic conflict is absent in Annis Stockton's use of religious matter in "Epistle—To Lucius," which idolizes its subject without the sort of impediments we have seen in the writings of Anne Bradstreet, Esther Burr, and Sarah Prince.

In contrast to Sarah, both Anne and Esther seem not to have brought to full consciousness their inclination to idolize a human exemplar. Esther, in particular, experienced difficulty in finding God in her heart, even when participating in the liberal Presbyterian celebration of the Lord's Supper; instead, the image of God (Sarah and Aaron) filled her emotional emptiness. Unknown to Esther, human companionship—intimate, loverlike—had become the surrogate religion of her heart. This is the unperceived idolatrous disposition veiled by Esther's dutiful allusion to Job in her guarded letter to her father. Had he detected it, Jonathan Edwards would have firmly censured his daughter's secret sense of self-validation through her latently idolatrous coalescence of friendship and authorship. Only Esther's soulmate Sarah knew. Only to Sarah did Esther confess her transgressive tendency to idolize friendship and authorship: "To tell the truth I love my self two [too] well to be indifferent whether I write or no" (89).

THREE

Captivity and Liberation

The instances of logonomic conflict we have reviewed to this point occur in works written by Congregationalist and Presbyterian authors. As my discussion peripherally indicates, these women are by no means perfectly aligned in every aspect of their Reformed beliefs. Mary English and Anne Bradstreet do not share precisely the same cultural heritage or, perhaps, Congregationalist ideas, which were far from monolithic even at the start of the Puritan enterprise in England (Foster 1991). And compared with Bradstreet and English, Esther Edwards Burr reflects a more liberating exposure to both Presbyterian dogma and eighteenth-century thought, while at the same time in some important respects she also seems, in contrast to them, less able to accommodate the validation of secular interests. Nevertheless, whether conservative or liberal, these authors collectively share a Calvinistic reading of existence and a Puritan context for coming to terms with their identity as women. It is not surprising, therefore, that their writings should mutually reflect similar problems in self-expression and aesthetics despite some variation in authorial contexts.

We turn now to two Quaker women—Elizabeth Hanson (1684-1737) and Elizabeth Ashbridge (1713-55)—to consider whether they were more successful in negotiating the theocratic logonomic system in which they lived. It is reasonable to raise this possibility because in many important respects Quaker women, in comparison to their Congregationalist and Presbyterian peers, enjoyed a greater opportunity for enhancing their self-esteem (Edkins 1980).

They found this opportunity within both the theological beliefs and the social structures of the Society of Friends.

Outside the Friends, of course, they were pariahs, as is attested by the well-known history of their persecution in many of the colonies. To their adversaries, Quaker women were whorish vagabonds, polluters of religious faith, and irrational opponents of both civil and ecclesiastical authority (Koehler 1980, 246-53). All of these charges readily converged in the handy suspicion that Quaker women routinely practiced witchcraft (288). Their adversaries often believed, in short, that male and female Quakers alike spoke in Satanic double-talk, not in Pentecostal tongues.

And speak they did, especially women, who found in Quakerism a communal legitimation of their voice. Similar to the early Christians, with whom the Quakers identified (Bowden 1850, 1:30), persecution from without strengthened communal bonding from within, even to the extent of encouraging the formation of a pantheon of Quaker martyrs. Within this community, Quaker women found an identity and voice unlike any offered by other colonial Christian sects. This greater liberation of female identity made Quakerism particularly attractive to women. For some women, it has been suggested (Koehler 1980, 258), Quakerism seems to have cured depression. More generally, however, it appealed to those who desired to breach some of the restraints placed upon their gender by the prevalent social structures of their day.

In fact, as was the case with Mary Fisher and Anne Austin (the first Quakers in the colonies, both jailed on the charge of witchcraft in 1656), Quaker women could serve as preachers, authorized to speak as men. During Oliver Cromwell's Protectorate, an apprehensive House of Commons affirmed that only officially ordained males may preach (Otten 1992, 358), but growing numbers of English Quaker women persisted in the practice and later even defended it in print. Such publications as Margaret Fell's *Womens Speaking Justified, Proved and Allowed of by the Scriptures* (1666, 1667), Anne Whitehead and Mary Elson's *An Epistle for True Love,*

Unity, and Order in the Church of Christ (1680), and Mary Waite's *Epistle from the Women's Yearly Meeting at New York* (1688) anticipated the many eighteenth-century defenses of the practice that were to follow, all of which advanced the early case made by George Fox.

Fox, the first major proponent of Quaker beliefs, pointed to scriptural examples of female preachers. He understood Saint Paul's equation of the sexes in Galatians to refer to the quotidian, not only to the afterlife, as we saw Congregationalist minister Cotton Mather insist in *Ornaments for the Daughters of Zion*. Fox did acknowledge Saint Paul's comment that "women keep silence in the churches: for it is not permitted unto them to speak" (1 Cor. 14:34), but unlike Mather, who cited this same passage specifically against female Quakers, Fox unconventionally interpreted the Pauline admonishment to refer only to ignorant women (Sewel 1800, 2:1636), women who had not been illuminated by the Inward Light, "the true Light, which lighteth every man" (John 1:9).

Since female Quakers were, in theory if not always in custom (Berkin 1996, 91-97), thoroughly equal to men, should not their writings transcend the kind of authoritarian dissonance evident in documents by contemporary Congregational and Presbyterian women? Not necessarily, as we shall see in this chapter on Hanson's captivity narrative and Ashbridge's autobiography. Although some features change, especially assumptions pertaining to gender parity, logonomic conflict nonetheless oddly surfaces at critical junctures in both Hanson's oral report and Ashbridge's transcribed account.

Given their view of female evangelizing, the dwindling but still prominent notion that public expression, especially writing, was principally a male province was not likely a significant constituent of the conflictive negotiation of orthodox and personal authority in works by female Quakers as it was for Bradstreet and Burr. We might reasonably surmise, however, that part of what these women tried to surmount—particularly the prevalent colonial view of women as the weaker sex and the Reformed theocratic devaluation of human attachments in general—constituted a kind of authoritarian static within their more "emancipated" contemplation of the Quaker idea of woman.

Elizabeth Hanson's Captivity Narrative

Elizabeth Hanson's *God's Mercy Surmounting Man's Cruelty* (1728) is today not the most well-known colonial captivity narrative, but it was sufficiently popular before 1800 to go through thirteen editions at home and various reprints abroad (Derounian-Stodola and Levernier 1993, 14). In later editions, of which there also were many, it was variously modified by others for both propagandistic and marketing purposes (VanDerBeets 1984, 16, 25-26). Whereas the American versions bear the initials "E.H.," the English editions are said to have been "taken in substance from her own mouth" by Samuel Bownas, a English Quaker divine. Bownas's actual role is uncertain, however. More certain is the claim of the first American edition to be a transcription of an earlier account written by a friend to whom Hanson told her story. Hanson, by her own admission "not . . . capable of keeping a journal" (Vaughan and Clark 1981, 244), was one of the many colonial women who could not write in the early eighteenth century.

Although the first American edition claims to "differ . . . very little from the original copy, but is even almost in her own words" (231), the "almost" insists that the published version is in fact a revision of the amanuensis's written account of the oral report. To be borne in mind, as well, is the eighteenth-century Quaker practice of collective authorship, an editorial procedure that "refines" Quaker works, including John Woolman's journal (Fichtelberg 1989, 77-80), to reflect ideal communal values. (The assumption that Hanson was a Quaker is based not only on Bownas's editorial presence in the English edition but also on her husband's religion and her explicit attack on Puritan clergy [q.v. Vaughan and Clark 1981, 241].) Such cautionary considerations about the fidelity of the text to Hanson's intention are important to remember when basing any argument on her report in its published form.

In spite of these reservations, the first American edition conveys, in narrative terms at least, a sense of overall authenticity. It is not polished in any literary way, a fact that might make the work seem uninspired to latter-day readers. The manner of its expression and design is minimalist, but this very same lack of embellishment and grace imparts a sense of genuineness to the book. Moreover, even if one or more Quaker editors possibly oversaw even the American document, they would in all likelihood not have interfered with Hanson's scriptural allusions, save perhaps to make them accurate. Even the private journals and personal letters of colonial women indicate, we should recall here, an extensive use of biblical allusion, especially the scriptural loci they encountered by way of the pulpit, discussion groups, and books. Accordingly, the biblical allusions in *God's Mercy Surmounting Man's Cruelty* are altogether likely Hanson's selections. And that they become sites of logonomic conflict similar in effect to those of her Congregationalist female peers further testifies on behalf of their authenticity as her own choices.

After having witnessed the slaying of two of her young children, Elizabeth Hanson, her two teenage daughters, her six-year-old son, and her maid were taken captive in Dover Township in August 1724, and forced to journey to French Canada. During the ordeal of this trek, Hanson's family sustained a series of further divisions. First her eldest daughter Sarah was "carried to another part of the country far distant from" her; then the captors "divided again, taking [her] second daughter [Elizabeth] and servant maid from" her (234-35). Before long, her "daughter and servant were likewise parted" (235). She would have lost the child born to her during this captivity had not tribal women aided her in preventing its starvation.

Hanson and her two remaining children are ransomed by a Frenchman, whose civility surprises her (given traditional English vilification of the French). She is reunited with her husband, who also eventually "recovers" the younger daughter. And she finally witnesses the successfulness of her husband's refusal "to omit anything for [the] redemption" of "his dear daughter Sarah," who is on the verge of being married to a young Native American. However, as

Hanson's family is painstakingly nearly reunited, it sustains one more substantial division. While seeking Sarah's liberation, her husband succumbs to an illness "in the wilderness" about "halfway between Albany and Canada" (243).

In short, the redemption of Hanson's family, its restoration to its wholeness prior to its traumatic rupture and subsequent divisions, never occurs. Two small children and a father are dead as a result of these events, and the remaining family members simply can never re-form the unit it once comprised. Hanson's family is, finally, at once reconstructed and fragmented, and this dichotomous condition henceforth defines the curious identity of her "redeemed" family.

Dichotomy likewise characterizes her overall response. On the surface, as the title of her little book indicates, she celebrates God's mercy in these providential events; below the surface, she unofficially registers an elegiac sense of loss akin to Bradstreet's in "Upon the Burning of Our House." The official, ventriloquized voice of praise observes, for example, that "though my own children's loss [of their father] is very great, yet I doubt not but his gain is much more" (243). Here the unauthorized, personal voice of mourning is evaded, consigned to the children (rather than herself) and to the anterior, the seemingly "left behind," portion of her figure of speech. In Hanson's use of *antithesis,* a neoclassical favorite for balancing one term against the other, proscribed sentiment appears to be prescriptively relinquished through the turn of a phrase. In a significant sense, of course, the ostensibly abandoned first part of this figure of speech (and its sentiment) lingers elegylike in the second part because the rhetorical play of the second part always depends on and points back to the first part for its effect and meaning.

A related interaction of public conviction and private sentiment can be detected more clearly when Hanson says at the end of her narrative that she "supplicat[es] the God and Father of all our mercies to be a father to [her] fatherless children" (243). To implore the Lord of mercy to serve as the father of the children, whom this same Lord mercilessly made fatherless, is an odd sentiment embodied here in a figure of speech (*ploce*) designed to negotiate Hanson's contrary feelings. The repetition of the word "father," commingling biblical and secular contexts, becomes a logonomic site subtly recording Hanson's resistant elegiac voice beneath the louder and more apparent expression of her acceptance of loss.

Sensitivity to this other voice here and in related instances in Hanson's book is stimulated by an indicative comment immediately preceding her unintentionally bivocal references to fatherhood: "I, therefore, desire and pray that the Lord will enable me patiently to submit to His will in all things" (243). Here her own sense of loss is not displaced, not attributed to her children. Here the conscious, official desire to submit counters an illegitimate desire to mourn. Hanson prays for patient acquiescence because by the end of her account she is apparently still unable to let go of the anterior, antithetical portion of her experience and narrative.

Earlier she had admitted her concern about "repining against God under [her] affliction"; at that time she "found it very hard to keep [her] mind as [she] ought under the resignation which is proper to be in under such afflictions and sore trials" (236). And this perfectly natural, if doctrinally illicit, response haunts the end of her tale when she speaks of needing divine empowerment if she is truly to resign herself to divine will. To grieve, after all, is not to submit to this will, for grieving is a form of resistance urged by unsanctioned sentiment. So at the close of her book the word "desire" becomes a site of conflict, a locus of an anxious negotiation of two opposite dispositions: resistant personal sorrow and submissive orthodox acceptance.

Hanson's desire for a sanctioned resignation she has yet to find not only calls attention to the experiential persistence of her grief but also erodes her narrational celebration of emancipation from coerced submission. In effect, her captivity narrative concludes in a mutually constitutive opposition: by praising God for liberating her from a captivity that separated her from her family; and, at the same time, by imploring God for a new captivity that would remove her from liberated, unlicensed feelings. If her family is not restored because all of its "divisions" cannot be temporally undone, if her precaptive state of mind is not restored because all of its dichotomous sentiments cannot be resolved, Hanson's captivity narrative likewise does not come full circle to restore her previous comfortable state of mind because it expresses a divided state of mind. Instead of restoration, in *God's Mercy Surmounting Man's Cruelty* one mode of bondage gives way to conditions that engender Hanson's earnest ache for another mode of captivity.

In this regard, Hanson's allusion to the Babylonian Captivity conveys more than she likely understood. During their wilderness trek, her daughter Sarah recites Psalm 137:1-3: "By the rivers of Babylon there we sat down, yea we wept when we remembered Zion; . . . there they that carried us away captives required of us a song" (233). Hope is communicated in this application of Scripture, hope to the effect that like the Jews under Cyrus (the conqueror of Babylon) the Hanson captives (likewise on the verge of "repining against God") will one day be freed from a "strange land" (Ps. 137:4) to return home and restore the temple of their previous confident faith. This is doubtless the analogy Hanson had in mind, although as we have seen at the end of her account, the comfort of both her home and her faith has not been fully recovered.

Indeed, it would seem—despite Hanson's probable ignorance of the detail—that the allusion aptly associates her final failure to escape the locus of her captivity (reinscribed through both an expressed concern with a lingering grief and a desire for a divinely imposed recapture) with those many Jews who never left Babylon after their emancipation. For them, as for the mourning part of Hanson's mind, the former theocratic home rather than the locality of captivity had become the strange land. The difference, of course, is that these Jews stayed voluntarily, whereas Hanson's continuing thralldom to grief in her life is as involuntary as is the persistent echo of Davidian lamentation throughout her narrative.

This issue of volition likewise emerges at a crucial moment of logonomic conflict in the final sentence of Hanson's book: "I have given a short but a true account of some of the remarkable trials and wonderful deliverances which I never purposed to expose but that I hope thereby the merciful kindness and goodness of God may be magnified, and the reader hereof provoked with more care and fear to serve Him in righteousness and humility, and then my designed end and purpose will be answered" (244). There is much here that is conventional, but of special interest is the allusion to Mary's canticle embracing her maternal role, replete with future sorrow, in the birth of Jesus: "My soul doth magnify the Lord" (Luke 1:46). This alignment with Mary, one far more comfortable for Hanson than it is for contemporaneous Congregationalist women, represents her conscious desire; at the same time, however, it peculiarly underscores a key difference between Elizabeth Hanson and Mary. Mary's submission is totally voluntary and achieved, whereas Elizabeth's is coerced and incomplete.

Hanson has not been given a choice as to whether or not she would play a role in a course of events that would result in the demise of her two children and her husband. She has, on the contrary, been given, and is expected to resign herself to, a providential fait accompli. As a result, the allusion to Mary's acquiescence to divine will is bivocal within the dual contexts of Hanson's narrative; it expresses Hanson's wish to conform to a licensed theocratic ideal of humility and voluntary submission, and it also inadvertently intimates another concurrent desire to align with an illicit personal sentiment of grief and its involuntary resistance to any renunciation of temporal loss.

It is, in fact, a curious feature of *God's Mercy Surmounting Man's Cruelty* that the language Hanson uses to describe her involuntary enslavement crosses over into the language she uses to describe her relationship with the deity. There is nothing typological or deliberate in this association; it is incidental and unwitting, albeit it possibly intimates Hanson's repressed personal sentiment. In response to her situation, Hanson fashions the following statements: "I must go or die. There was no resistance" (Vaughan and Clark 1981, 232); "This was a sore grief to us all. But we must submit" (234); "I dreaded the tragical design of my master" (237). These remarks refer to her Native American captors, but aside from their specific textual emplacement, these remarks are strikingly similar to her sense of both "having no other way but to cast [her] care upon God" and "the overruling power of Him in whose Providence [she] put [her] trust" (239). No wonder that at the end of her narrative she seeks a new form of captivity, seeks to be made "to submit to His will in all things"; for given the danger to the spiritual life of her soul occasioned by rebellious bitter feelings of resistant grief, once again she "must go or die. There was no resistance."

Hanson is doubtless straightforward when she openly declares her "designed end and purpose" as the stimulation of her reader's humble submission (like Mary's) to a God of "merciful deliverance[s]" (239). Nevertheless, the elegiac voice lingering throughout her account, and inadvertently countering the primary theme of God's "merciful kindness and goodness," implies a different "end and purpose." At moments of dichotomizing logonomic conflict, such as the allusion to Mary's voluntary willingness to magnify the Lord through submission, Hanson's bivocality includes another story altogether, a story she can barely articulate. This story concerns not the physical miseries she endured, but specifically the mental "afflictions [that] are not to be set forth in words to the extent of them" (236). They cannot be so "set forth" because the feelings they arouse surpass the capacity of language and, more important, are theocratically prohibited.

This illegitimate other story, as fatherless as Hanson's children, concerns lost sweetness and found bitterness. This underground version of her tale opposes the orthodox moral extracted from such an observation as "None knows what they can undergo till they are tried, for what I had thought in my own family not fit for food would here have been a dainty dish and sweet morsel" (238). The moral analogue for this passage surfaces earlier in Hanson's report when, apropos the captives being given pieces of old beaver skin to eat, she cites Proverbs 27:7: "to the hungry soul every bitter thing is sweet" (234). Contemplating the demise of her husband, she publicly asserts this sweetness—"his gain is much more"—while she

privately husbands "the bitterness of death" (237). Before her captivity, she had not been hungry in either her physical or spiritual
life. After her experiences in the wilderness, she indeed has become
a hungry soul who laments the loss of her husband and who consequently requires divine force to make her accept "the bitterness of
death." For Hanson, if we listen to her faint outlawed voice, the
bitterness of dispossession in her life has hardly been translated into
a gracious sweetness in her soul, even as the end of her captivity
has hardly resulted in the "sweet" restoration of her family life or
the "gracious" resolution of her narrative. Hanson may have wished
to endorse the words that immediately follow Mary's express choice
to magnify the Lord—"He hath filled the hungry with good things"
(Luke 1:46)—but certain embedded resistant features of her experience and her story insist otherwise.

Although Hanson is a Quaker, the effects we have reviewed in
her book are similar to those in the well-known captivity narrative
by Congregationalist Mary Rowlandson (c. 1635-post 1678).
Rowlandson's *Sovereignty and Goodness of God* (1682) likewise evidences an undeclared tension between the experience of woe and
its displacement through sanctioned moral representation (Breitwieser 1990, 10; Logan 1993). There are, as well, moments of
logonomic conflict, especially when the Bible is cited. Such moments contain unidentified discrepancies between what actually
happens and what is quoted by way of explanation. As a result, although Rowlandson (like Hanson) alludes to the Bible in an orthodox manner to analogize her situation, "her complicated use of
Scripture reveals both a fear and an anger at a punishing God that
must be transformed into an anger at herself, which nonetheless
resurfaces as a paradoxically self-abnegating accusation of Him"
(Toulouse 1992, 664). And similar to Hanson's manner, this complex effect is apparently not intentional: "The more mechanically
Rowlandson acknowledges her submission in orthodox terms, the
more she complicates the range of explanation offered to her by
such orthodoxy"; "as hard as she might try to conceal it in her *Narrative,* the text reveals the impasse imposed upon her imagination

by her own interrogation of the old models for establishing her sense of value" (669).

Hanson's oral report of her captivity is a work of less imagination than is Rowlandson's written document. Nevertheless, despite different religious orientations and slight editing by other hands, both works are equally rich in documenting certain problems with the authorization of personal sentiment and expression that were frequently experienced by female colonial authors, including Quakers.

Elizabeth Ashbridge's Autobiography

Some Account of the Fore Part of the Life of Elizabeth Ashbridge (written, c. 1753; 1st ed., 1774) is a far more complex Quaker testament than is *God's Mercy Surmounting Man's Cruelty.* Ashbridge's narrative, which we have only in others' transcriptions, recounts the numerous trials of a young woman who eloped at the age of fourteen and within months found herself widowed, exiled from her family home, and badly prepared to survive either in the world or in her mind. Her education, which had depended "mostly on [her] Mother," had primarily emphasized "the principles of virtue" (Shea 1990, 147); but in the world of economic exchange in which she now had become a bound servant, virtue seemed virtually valueless. Virtue's residual value, moreover, was readily bankruptable, even merely by calumnious words: "I began to think my Credit was gone (for they said many things of me which I blessed God were not True)" (153). Indentured physically and adrift emotionally, teenager Elizabeth is brought to the brink of suicide more than once during her tribulations in New York.

Ashbridge characterizes her experiences collectively as various forms of bondage. This metaphor pertains not only to her "becoming bound" through indentured "Servitude" (151), the abject conditions of which are similarly documented by Elizabeth Sprigs, Ashbridge's southern contemporary. The metaphor of bondage also represents Ashbridge's second marriage, of which she says, "I got released from one cruel Servitude & then not Contented got into another" (153-54). During this marriage, the itinerancy of her new husband was hardly the only "Disagreeable" matter to which she felt she "must submit" (155). Such experiences of servility, however, had an important antecedent, which Ashbridge seems reticent to declare openly but which her memoir associates with her later replications of thralldom: her constraining relationship with her father.

As was typical of early-eighteenth-century colonial daughters, Elizabeth was not free to decide much for herself, including her marriage. She explicitly admits that her courtship with the first young man she would marry was "without [her] Parents' consent," that her impetuous marriage to him was an act of "disobedience," and that her behavior had denied her parents the "right . . . to have disposed of [her] to their contents" (Shea 1990, 148). When she eloped with her first husband, she in effect dispossessed her parents, particularly her father, of the property of her body. Her act was a violation not only of filial respect but also of economic propriety concerning children, an issue as well in eighteenth-century representations of rape as a confiscation of patriarchal property (Williams 1993). Dispossessed of what was by custom rightfully his, Elizabeth's father "was so displeased," he "would not send for" her and "would do nothing for" her (148). Henceforth she was not only widowed but also orphaned. She was sheltered briefly by relatives and eventually turned loose in the world. Although some time later her father relented and apparently would have met the financial obligations of her indenture, Elizabeth "chose Bondage rather" than to return to his household (153), and she even desperately entertained the possibility of running off with an acting troupe.

Elizabeth presents her "Disobedience in marrying" (153), her tenuous rebellion against her father, as a kind of fall from grace. (The word "disobedience" is virtually a refrain in the first part, as the word "obedience" is in the second part of all versions of her account.) Insubordination serves as a primary determinant of the harrowing experiences that befall her in a harsh world where, subsequent to her postlapsarian expulsion from the security of her family home, widowed virtue can purchase little, if anything, and presumably can be forfeited by mere verbal deceit. As presented in all the versions of her narrative, her life in the world commences with and replicates this self-wounding insurrection against thralldom to her father. As best she is able, accordingly, she resists her inhumane master, who purchased her indenture; her stern father, who eventually relented and would permit her to return on his terms; and her domineering second husband, who "flew into a rage" and "Struck [her] with sore Blows" when she announced her willingness "to obey all his Lawfull Commands but where they Imposed upon [her] Conscience" (165-66). (Anticipating a prevalent custom today in marriage ceremonies, incidentally, Quaker women for some time have not agreed to obey their husbands [Frost 1973, 174].)

Ashbridge's coalescence of her original disobedience and her a posteriori acts of resistance to male authority include a significant revision of her stance toward the orthodox ministry. In her sheltered youth, she had looked upon the clergy as paragons of male empowerment in the world, so much so that she "sometimes wept with Sorrow, that [she] was not a boy [so] that [she] might have" become a minister (Shea 1990, 148). (This sentiment is expressed even more passionately, and hence possibly more authentically, in the variant report that she "sometimes grieved at . . . not being a boy" [Baym 1994, 602].) While adrift in the world, however, she becomes skeptical toward "that set of men," the "Very Religious" for whom "in [her] youth" she "had a Great Veneration" (152). Later still, she sees "beyond the Men made Ministers," those "Mercenary creatures" more devoted to "the Love of Money" than to "the regard of Souls" (163).

This repudiation of the traditional ministry amounts in effect to Ashbridge's ultimate defiance of male authority, a defiance she crowns by becoming a Quaker preacher. Ashbridge fulfills her youthful fantasy of becoming a minister by way of inversion. Far past the point of wishing she were a male so that she could join the traditional ministry, she now identifies with an unorthodox ministry in which women and men are equally "ordained" solely through their encounter with the Inward Light. And, Ashbridge's account further suggests, these Quaker preachers redeem the establishmentarian Christian ministry by displacing the male mercenary interest of such conformist clergy with a "female" alternative interest in the heretofore dispossessed principles of virtue (of the kind she learned from her mother).

This version of the plot of her autobiography reinforces a recent observation that Ashbridge records "the phenomenon of a woman speaking of her coming to speak" or, in other words, her progression from speechless listening to numerous voices to her proclamation of a "new identity . . . through the familiar Quaker usage of 'thee'" (Shea 1990, 132-33). But, as we shall observe, a specter-like question haunts this progress toward empowerment of voice, despite an authorizing belief in the Inward Light. This question challenges the "narrative restraint" that has been esteemed as "admirable" (Shea 1968, 37).

In fact, a key point in the loose structure of the autobiography provides an apt place to initiate an investigation of this instability in referential authority. In terms of this structure, Ashbridge's search for voice may be schematized as evincing a V configuration:

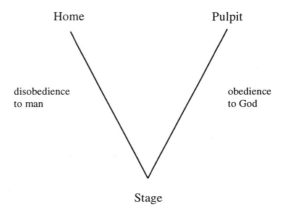

At first, the trajectory of Ashbridge's experiences inclines downward. Unable to return home, she becomes a nearly powerless and voiceless indentured servant, a nondescript human whose beliefs (including her religious faith) are so unstable that she becomes despondent and suicidal. At the nadir of this downward turn lies a temptation, "another Snare," which "would Probably have been [her] Ruin." Here she is temporarily "Perswaded" to join a "Play house company then at New York" (153), indeed a temptation given the shared Congregationalist, Presbyterian, and Quaker association of theater productions and players with unchaste behavior and bad reputations, specifically in violation of the seventh commandment (Meserve 1977, 26-27).

The earliest contributors to these Reformed sects apparently did not construct the stage in these terms; in a work revered by these sects and commonly designated as *Book of the Martyrs* (English version, 1563), for instance, John Foxe associates "players, printers, [and] preachers" as allies "set up of God, as a triple bulwark" against the antiChrist (Foxe 1965, 6:57). But with the emergence of the new theater, the stage and the Reformed pulpit became antagonists in defining the nature of spirituality (Knapp 1993). By Ashbridge's time, Quakers spoke of the theater as the "floodgate of vice," especially "looseness and immorality," and they consequently influenced eighteenth-century laws against theatrical productions in Pennsylvania (Bowden 1854, 2:287-89).

As a naive teenager, Ashbridge is enticed by the theater, which evidently appealed to a number of other young women, most notably late in the eighteenth century, as a flagrant opportunity to invert the social paradigm of female impotence, invisibility, and silence (Dudden 1994). Ashbridge is attracted by the disingenuous promise that with membership in the troupe she would "Live Like a Lady" (153). Implied in this promise is the notion that the deception of on-stage representation could be transferred to the off-stage world, certainly an appealing proposition for such a luckless child as she was at that time. However, as suggested by the retrospective reference to her predictable "Ruin," many of young

Elizabeth's adult contemporaries would have readily detected a shady nuance, an allusion to prostitution, in the euphemistic expression "Live Like a Lady." Ashbridge reads numerous plays in preparation for joining the troupe, but finally she resists this temptation after "Consider[ing] what [her] Father would say" now that he has "forgiven [her] Disobedience in marrying" (Shea 1990, 153).

Eventually Ashbridge remarries, which frees her from her indenture if not altogether from theatrical performances, for she has married a man who is attracted to her for her dancing (154) and who, in a demonstration of his hostility to her Quaker leanings, makes her "the Spectacle & discourse of [his] Company" in a tavern (162). If her marriage binds her in ways similar to her indenture—as she herself claims—it nonetheless results in encounters that collectively form the upward movement of her life. Ashbridge affirms that through the debilitating itinerancy of her husband "God [brought] unforeseen things to Pass, for by [her] going . . . [she] was brought to [the] Knowledge of [divine] Truth" (158). In terms of the structural scheme of her memoir, that is to say, she finds fulfillment in a new community where, as a Quaker preacher, she displaces corrupt father figures. Instead of participating in the false spectacle of voicing some humanly authored dramatic text and experiencing an illusory freedom under the controlling gaze of male spectators (akin to her later experience in a tavern), she now participates in the genuine drama of voicing a divinely authored providential text. Like other Quaker "Ministers . . . [likewise] dipt into all States, that thereby they might be able to Speak to all Conditions" (168), Ashbridge reconfigures theatricality so that the pulpit of her adult female ministry inverts/reconverts the stage demarcating the nadir of her youthful experiences.

Such an inversion, or reconversion, is meant to be as heuristic as are the official dichotomies (as opposed to the conflictive sentiments) of Hanson's captivity narrative. And on first encounter the redemptive message of inversion seems as definitively conclusive as Ashbridge apparently intended. On second thought, however, the trope of the stage steadfastly inheres within Ashbridge's implied reconstruction of it as the pulpit, just as mourning persists as a subversive undercurrent within Hanson's use of antithesis when speaking of her acceptance of divine will. (Ashbridge does not explicitly refer to a preacher's platform, which is not a usual feature of Quaker worship; but since the pulpit would likely be mentally imaged by most non-Quaker readers of her day whenever they encountered her references to preaching, it is an implicit contemporary metonymy for all the forums of her own ministry, including her memoir.) Ashbridge's oral and written preaching, like stage performances, are modes of theatricality, spectacles that cannot break free from what they once were culturally aligned with (as John Foxe suggested in 1563) and what they now invert or reconvert. Although in the autobiography the allegedly immoral stage may be superseded by the moral pulpit, the displaced stage persists as a palimpsest beneath this implicit pulpit. And, correspondingly, the practice of assuming and discarding various identities on the stage, including clever transgressions of gender boundaries, informs and latently destabilizes Ashbridge's depiction of her unconventional identity as a *female* preacher at the end of her memoir. How firm, and how firmly authorized, is such an identity if it is troped, however accidentally, in proscribed theatrical terms?

This is a literary not a religious query. But interestingly the semiotic equivocation suggested by Ashbridge's tacit reinscription of the metaphor of theatricality is also replicated in her management of her more overtly declared subject of disobedience. As we established earlier, Ashbridge coalesces her "fathering" act of disobedience and her subsequent acts of obedience to God through resistance to male authority, acts that collectively result in inversions of stage/pulpit theatricality and male/female ministry. As presented by Ashbridge, then, disobedience is bi-valent. It is, in other words, referentially unstable since it may produce good as well as bad effects. Left unasked, because the answer would become enmeshed in the vexatious issue of authority, is a key question: how is one—especially the *second* or *weaker* sex as defined in colonial times—to know when disobedience is appropriate?

This question of authorization is faintly inscribed, if finally un-readable, beneath the equivocal opening of the autobiography. In the very first sentence Ashbridge claims that some of the "uncommon Occurrences" in her life were "through disobedience brought upon" herself, while "others . . . were for [her] Good" (147). Such a comment at once authorizes and deauthorizes disobedience, at least certain instances of disobedience. But which instances? The insubordination she directs at her master, at her second husband, and at mercenary ministers seems sufficiently clear, but it does not mask fully the prior defiance of her father, the oft confessed bad act that somehow leads to Ashbridge's salvation. Nor does the V-like symmetry of her plot—how the disobedience to her human father of the first part leads to her decline outside of her home and how the obedience to the divine father in the second part leads to her ascent to the pulpit—quite disguise the problem.

Indeed, an attempt to fashion from Ashbridge's memoir a moral map, as it were, based on her specific references to disobedience and obedience would result in a substantial confusion of vectoring. Obscured in the shadowy margins of this confusion is the issue of authority concerning how to recognize improper disobedience from proper disobedience, heuristic reproach from homiletic commemoration, especially when assessing one's own life. In this regard, at least, it is more of a mystification of the problem than a clarification to be told, as we previously heard, that "God brings unforeseen things to Pass," that "unforeseen things are brought to Pass, by a Providential hand" (158, 164).

The doctrine of the Inward Light, of interior divine revelation, is the official Quaker repository for negotiating this problem. Nevertheless, the *narrative* function of proper and improper disobedience in Ashbridge's account, from its ambiguous opening sentence onward, defies conclusive resort to such a closeting doctrinal rationale in this instance. History, moreover, attests to what complications can emerge from antinomian attempts to harken to an inner voice, and Ashbridge's document concurs. This memoir progresses from her youthful "giving way to a foolish passion" when she elopes

(148), through inner promptings to hang herself (153), to receiving divine messages "as tho' [she] had heard a Distinct Voice" (167). In narrative terms, as distinct from religious ones, a Bakhtinian heteroglossia (Holquist 1981, 428) lingers in the memoir, specifically a polyphony of competing inner provocations. In narrative terms, a confessional moment at midpoint in her account suggests the magnitude of this polyphony. There she admits how easy it is for her and others to mistake the voice of "the Subtile Serpent," when as an interior prompter he "hiddenly" interprets "the Texts of Scripture," as if his influence were "a timely Caution from a good Angel" (159). Although Ashbridge plots her story so that her youthful disobedience to her human father is redressed by "the fruits of [her adult] Obedience" to the divine father (167), she cannot repair the implicit confounding of authority that inheres in this very pattern, whereby improper disobedience leads to proper obedience. Contingently negotiating this crisis in authority, in short, Ashbridge's particular application of the disobedience/obedience equation is as "fatherless" as Hanson's particular application of the bitterness/sweetness equation.

The fragility of Ashbridge's construction of a plot in which proscribed disobedience is transformed into prescribed obedience, prohibited stage is transformed into the licensed pulpit, is likewise suggested by an incident reported near the conclusion of her autobiography. At this point she tells of "hearing a Woman relate a book she had read in which it was Asserted that Christ was not the son of God," merely "the Contrivance of men." Immediately "an horrour of Great Darkness fell upon [her], which Continued for three weeks" (167). Ashbridge's response is surprising given the advanced stage of her Quaker beliefs at this juncture. Could this woman's message, temporarily marring the heuristic plot of the narrative, inadvertently suggest a certain ambiguity in the design of Ashbridge's textualized life and theatrical memoir?

Consider that the opposition between this woman and Ashbridge is determined merely by inversion, the very same narrative device of Elizabeth's life and her autobiography as a whole. The two women are like opposite sides of the same coin. If Ashbridge's autobiography represents the assertion of self as authorized by its alignment with divine authority, the reading woman represents the supplanting of divine authority by the assertive self as the sole fashioner of the notion of divinity. Ashbridge's extensive incapacitation upon hearing this woman's views possibly indicates Ashbridge's unconscious acknowledgment of the ambiguity inherent in her personal reliance upon the precarious disobedience-obedience formula.

Such moments, I am inclined to believe, hint at Ashbridge's unwitting anxiety over the issue of authority; the failure of sanctioned obedience to displace altogether illicit disobedience and of the pulpit to displace altogether the stage in the autobiography corresponds to the failure of Ashbridge's attained voice (identity) to displace altogether her initial voicelessness. This observation indeed may seem very strange, especially in light of the trajectory of her life toward the pulpit. A closer consideration of her voice, however, suggests a distinctive complexity in this matter.

When Ashbridge disobeys in the first part of her memoir, she expresses herself through the authority of her passionate feelings for her first husband. But this self-expression, explicitly designated as illegitimate disobedience, is dispossessed of its authority and replaced by divinely inspired self-expression, explicitly designated as legitimate obedience: "[God] would require me to go forth & declare to others what he . . . had done for my Soul" (160). The latter is, however, a form of ventriloquism, as if on the world stage she were a player delivering lines from a divinely crafted script (Scripture). Her self-expression, in other words, is from her point of view authorized from an *inward* prompting determined by an *outward* divine force. In this sense, therefore, her speech is not, or at least not entirely, a form of self-expression. The voicelessness Ashbridge believes has been transformed into identity-giving voice has not at last been fully displaced. When she disqualifies her early personal feelings as unauthorized and credits her new beliefs as authorized, her voice is at once empowered on the basis of external license (God) and disempowered on the basis of internal license (sentiment). As a plot element, the conversion of voicelessness to voice remains, finally, as entangled in ambiguity as is the correspondent and implicated conversion of disobedience into obedience, stage into pulpit, male into female ministry.

This curiously equivocated sense of identity, particularly in terms of an inversion of gender roles, informs another key moment in Ashbridge's narrative. Here she reports one of her dreams, which combines several biblical allusions and provides a remarkable site of logonomic conflict:

> I had a Dream, & tho' some make a ridicule of Dreams, yet this seemed a significant one to me & therefore [I] shall mention it. I thought somebody knocked at the Door, by which when I had opened it there stood a Grave woman, holding in her right hand an oil lamp burning, who with a Solid Countenance fixed her Eyes upon me & said—"I am sent to tell thee that If thou'l return to the Lord thy God, who hath Created thee, he will have mercy on thee, & thy Lamp shall not be put out in obscure darkness;" upon which the Light flamed from the Lamp in an extraordinary Manner, & She left me and I awoke. [Shea 1990, 153]

This passage may be read, as it has been (131), as a prophecy of the narrator's eventual discovery of both "the Quaker Inner Light" and "an achieved identity." Also encoded in this dream, however, are conflictive elements concerning the nature and enablement of this identity.

The dream combines several biblical allusions. The last part of the prophecy echoes a scriptural admonition, that "the lamp of the wicked shall be put out," that "whoso curseth his father or his mother, his lamp shall be put out in obscure darkness" (Prov. 13:9 and 20:20). In terms of the latter passage, Ashbridge's vision evidently reassures her that she has been forgiven for her specific transgression against her parents—another clue, incidentally, to the problematic importance of her primary act of disobedience to the salvational outcome of her life. The dream as well alludes to those

New Testament passages promising, for instance, that the followers of Jesus, as "the light of the world[,] . . . shall not walk in darkness, but shall have the light of life" (John 8:12).

Still more prominent in the dream is the scriptural text that advises Christians, "Let . . . your lights [be] burning" when the "Lord . . . cometh and knocketh" (Luke 12:35-36). In renderings of this scene—images of which Quakers would not have approved but which Ashbridge may have seen in books or while living abroad, especially among Roman Catholics—Christ holds a lamp in one hand while knocking on a door with the other.

Most interesting in the dream version of this scene is the transmutation of the gender of the light-bearing visitant at the door. This unacknowledged feature is far more significant than the acknowledged dubiety of dreams, the latter factor accommodated by Ashbridge's use of the equivocal word "seemed" in order to justify the inclusion of the vision in her account. The person in the dream is not Jesus or even John, who spoke of himself as a "witness of the Light, that all men through him might believe" (John 1:6). It is a woman with a grave countenance. In one sense, this figure usurps the male savior role, as a prominent colonial cultural feature, but unwittingly it also displaces John and Jesus as well. The figure *may* represent Ashbridge's attempt to awaken herself from her subjection to suicidal nonidentity as a commodity in a mercenary world controlled by men. Read as a projection of her later ministerial role as an ambassador of Christ, the woman in her dream seems a bold, even heretical, figuring of an achievable autonomous identity.

Beneath this fantasy of self-awakening, however, the woman in the dream derives her dramatic power by appearing in a scene and role given signification by someone prior to herself. In other words, the somber woman (like an actress in a theatrical performance) replays, but does not invent, a role in the dream. Her inversion/transformation of the role cannot break free from its antecedents anymore than can obedience from disobedience, the pulpit from the stage, or female from male ministry throughout Ashbridge's memoir. The grave woman's performance invokes the memory of and draws its own power from another, antecedent, and far more potent one: the image of Christ bearing the light of truth and knocking on our door. So, finally, if on first impression the scene seems an assertion of female selfhood that unwittingly displaces even Jesus, on second impression it is only a satellite reenactment of a biblical depiction. This biblical image inheres as an authorizing palimpsest beneath the more visible meanings of the dream, meanings always dependent on this submerged authority.

The reversal of gender is likewise equivocated in the dream. The female image of self-awakening (self-authorization) is also ultimately authorized from without by a male prototype. That is to say, female transgression (self-motivated disobedience) is also ultimately commissioned by conformity (obedience) to a male model, whether John's or Jesus'.

The logonomic conflict evident in this dream serves as an index to the dilemma Ashbridge faced as an mid-eighteenth-century woman seeking self-definition through personal expression. The paradox informing this dream is a microcosm of the entire pattern of her search for identity, founded on an illegitimate disobedience against her father, that culminates in her obedient arrogation of the male role of ministers and of the power they wield through spoken and written language. In the scheme of her story she tries to transform one thing into its opposite, an act that paradoxically unites and disunites contraries. She tries to warrant obedience to herself by means of obedience to God. But this equation is hardly equal in its parts, for as Ashbridge observes on another occasion, "if it be of God [you] can't over throw it, & if it be of your self it will soon fall" (167). In the dynamic of Ashbridge's implied equation, obedience to God necessarily overdetermines obedience to herself, and so they finally are not at all equitable.

Ashbridge achieves identity and voice, less from an internal authority than from an external authority. This means, despite her mystifying acknowledgment (like Hanson's) that God "Makest every bitter thing Sweet" (170), that *to some degree* the authority of her voice and identity remains firmly indentured. Ashbridge inadvertently reinscribes indenture in *Some Account,* just as Hanson reinscribes captivity in *God's Mercy Surmounting Man's Cruelty.* Their narratives dramatize, finally, an anxious, conflicted, and unresolved negotiation of authorization, expressed through the dynamic interplay of the dichotomous inversions and reconversions composing the mutual "plot" of their lives.

FOUR

Subjection and Prophecy

The critical response to the poetry of Phillis Wheatley (c. 1754-84) often registers disappointment or surprise. Some critics have complained that the verse of this African American slave is insecure (Collins 1975, 78), imitative (Richmond 1974, 54-66), and incapacitated (Burke 1991, 33, 38)—at worst, the "product of a White mind" (Jamison 1974, 414-15) and the "barter of [the poet's] soul" (Richmond 1982, 127). Others, in contrast, have applauded Wheatley's critique of Anglo-American discourse (Kendrick 1993, 222-23), her revision of literary models and acknowledgment of African heritage (Watson 1996), and her verification of selfhood (Baker 1991, 39-41). Readers have observed critiques of slavery in her use of classical tradition and irony (Shields 1993), especially in her elegies (Levernier 1993). In her verse relying on the tradition of epistolary praise practiced by Alexander Pope, moreover, she strategically motivated her contemporary readers to acquiesce to her abolitionist position so that they would be the recipients of her acclaim rather than her ironic correction (Willard 1995). And some readers have specifically discerned various languages of escape in her poetry, each similarly extracted from the traditions of Western culture (Davis 1953; Erkkila 1993; O'Neale 1986). In her poems on religion, death, and art, such critics have argued, Wheatley attained a certain amount of freedom. Especially noteworthy is a mode of liberation occasionally evident in her use of "double meaning and ambiguity," both designed for "the close reader of [her] poems" (Matson 1982, 119). Indeed, Wheatley was keenly sensitive to her potential readership and, as a result, apparently managed her self-presentation with an eye to the marketplace (Felker 1994).

Wheatley's use of ambiguity, it is reasonable to suspect, was partially influenced by her exposure to Enlightenment thinking on human rights and abolitionist theory. This exposure came primarily from the pulpit. Insofar as we know, Wheatley attended the New South Congregational Church, where her owners worshiped. By 1771, she had become an active member of the Old South Congregational Church in Boston. At that time the clergy, including those with whom Wheatley had contact (Levernier 1991, 23), integrated religious and political concerns in their sermons (Weber 1988, 5-13). Also from the pulpit, in conjunction with her personal reading and her discussions with others, Wheatley became familiar with select eighteenth-century Protestant commentaries on Scripture and with approved secular applications of biblical passages as well. Doubtless she was very attentive to these exegeses, for familiarity with Scripture ranked very high in importance for eighteenth-century African Americans generally (Brown 1996, 233) and the King James version of the Bible was, among a handful of other favorite books, specifically prized by Wheatley in particular.

Scripture, in fact, profoundly influenced her writings (Mason 1989, 15-16), as it did African American culture in general. Wheatley participated in the African American tradition of using Scripture as materia medica, as a therapeutic means of revising and transforming social reality (Smith 1994, 18). Wheatley engaged this tradition whenever the Bible provided her with devices for undercutting colonial assumptions about race (O'Neale 145). Wheatley's dual encounter with theological and secular applications of Holy Writ accounts for the compatibility of her religious and her political writings (Akers 1975; Burroughs 1974), a feature that anticipates a pattern in later African American literature (Hubbard 1994, 18-25). This double exposure encouraged her to relate evangelical Protestantism to both Revolutionary patriotism and romance neoclassicism. Such combinations in her writings, as Phillip M. Richards's investigations indicate, occupy a liminal space of transformed social position where Wheatley rewrites marginality, exults in spiritual equality, and urges her audience to rethink its inherited ideologies.

Wheatley's mingling of evangelicalism and patriotism occasionally included her resistance to slavery. Such a moment occurs in "On the Death of General Wooster" (1777), a Revolutionary War poem written four years after the poet's manumission. In this elegy, Wheatley forthrightly asks: how can citizens of the emergent American nation expect their freedom to prevail against tyranny "While yet (O deed ungenerous!) they disgrace / And hold in bondage Afric's blameless race?" (Mason 1989, 171). The sentiment expressed in this poem is also present, albeit much less explicitly, in such earlier verse as "To the Right Honourable William, Earl of Dartmouth" (1773). This poem proceeds guardedly in an elliptical manner akin to the kind of narrative blank that can potentially "stimulate the process of ideation" (Iser 1978, 111-12). The verse addressed to the Earl of Dartmouth elliptically associates "wanton Tyranny," which "enslave[s] the [colonial] land," with the "tyrannic" kidnapping of the poet as a child, an experience that fostered her "love of Freedom" (Mason 1989, 83).

Wheatley's attitude toward slavery did not change in the interval between these two poems. What changed was her social status, her emancipation from bondage. In the Wooster elegy she felt free to speak overtly against slavery, in contrast to her covert approach to the subject in her early verse. Throughout her career, Wheatley believed that slavery did not "find / Divine acceptance with th' Almighty mind" (Mason 171).

In several of her early poems, moreover, Wheatley specifically turns to Scripture to suggest the deity's aversion to slavery. In "On Being Brought from Africa to America," for instance, the direct celebration of her personal delight in Christianity includes a restrained, if resistant, "second voice" speaking subtly through two allusions to the Book of Isaiah. As presented by Wheatley's appropriated ministerial voice, these allusions rebuke Christian slave owners. The logonomic conflict resulting from Wheatley's use of biblical allusion in this manner differs from the examples presented in the preceding chapters, for it gives the impression of being a conscious choice, a deliberate construction designed to register the poet's underground renunciation of slavery. She evidently believed that this response was supported by the Bible.

Before describing the technique of "On Being Brought from Africa to America" in more detail, there are two neglected verse paraphrases by Wheatley that are apt precursors to this discussion. As the writings of Jane Colman Turell and Martha Wadsworth Brewster typify, verse paraphrases of Scripture, especially the Psalms, appealed to many colonial women authors. Wheatley's "Goliath and Garth" (a paraphrase of 1 Sam. 17) was announced in the 1772 proposal for her book, whereas her even more ambitious "Isaiah LXIII. 1-8" was not listed in the proposal. These two verse paraphrases, both included in *Poems on Various Subjects, Religious and Moral* (1773), may initially appear to be unlikely places to observe Wheatley's management of logonomic conflict. Critics, in fact, have shown very little interest in them. Both, however, are nuanced works worth a second look. They not only provide insight into the poet's manner in "On Being Brought from Africa to America"; they also evidence an artistic performance barely glimpsed by most readers of Wheatley's poetry.

"Goliath and Garth"

"Goliath and Garth," a recent reader has observed, suggests that Wheatley identifies with David as a servant of humble origin and as a lyricist from a distant land (Foster 1993, 41). We might speculate further that the emphasis on David's ruddy complexion in the chapter (1 Sam. 17:42) paraphrased by Wheatley, and in the preceding chapter (1 Sam. 16:12), also may have encouraged her to identify with the psalmist. Ruddiness, a reddish facial coloration signifying health, is not attributed to any other historical figure in Scripture. As a woman of color in predominantly white Boston, Wheatley may have found the biblical David appealing as a poet of divine favor whose distinctive skin pigmentation made him, as it were, a marked minority figure among his people.

If we accept the reasonable proposition that Wheatley identified with David, then we must ask why she focused on this scriptural passage concerning the psalmist rather than some other one. In response to this query, it is pertinent to note that the biblical text featured in her poem records David's emergence from obscurity. Possibly, then, he seemed a holy type for Wheatley's own anticipated movement from private life to public view. Nevertheless, we still must reckon with the role of combat in this particular biblical text. An emphasis on combat may seem unexpected, perhaps inappropriate, in the work of a poet frequently understood to be adaptive, sometimes even submissive, in reaction to her colonial environment.

Still more surprising is the fact that the militaristic feature of this scriptural passage is enhanced by Wheatley. Just as she invents an angel for the scene (Robinson 1984, 100), she also embellishes the details of both David's encounter with Goliath and Saul's rout of the Philistines. Whereas, for instance, Scripture reports that David's "stone sunk into his [Goliath's] forehead" (1 Sam. 17:49), Wheatley imagines that the stone "pierc'd the skull, and shatter'd all the brain" (Mason 1989, 65). Whereas Scripture reports that "the men of Israel and of Judah arose, and shouted, and pursued the Philistines . . . the wounded of [whom] fell down by the way" (1 Sam. 17:52), Wheatley envisions "scenes of slaughter" and "seas of blood": "There Saul thy thousands grasp'd th' impurpled sand / In pangs of death" (Mason 1989, 66). Wheatley's intensified dramatization stresses combat as the means of victory over the Philistines and as the means of David's emergence from obscure servitude in Saul's court.

Servitude is indeed a central issue in the Samuel passage. As Goliath indicates, if he is slain the Philistines will become the victor's "servants"; if he prevails, on the other hand, the vanquished will "serve" the Philistines (1 Sam. 17:9). Following this scriptural emphasis, Wheatley's paraphrase likewise specifies the outcome of the confrontation as "Perpetual service from the vanquish'd land" (Mason 1989, 61). Thinking about Wheatley's heightening of the scene of combat in her paraphrase, some might detect a displacement of her anger toward those who have enslaved her race, perhaps even a fantasy of retribution vicariously and safely expressed through a dramatic reenactment of her scriptural hero's remarkable feat.

Whatever the viability of such a reading in psychological terms, another interpretation is encouraged by the standard eighteenth-century Protestant scriptural commentaries on this episode in David's life. Such official interpretations of the Bible were primarily disseminated from the pulpit, which was likely the main source of Wheatley's knowledge about the passages she paraphrased. Concerning the Samuel passage treated by Wheatley, Protestant commentaries specify that the future king of the Israelites did not need a sword because he came, in David's own words, "in the name of the Lord," who "saveth not with [the] sword" (1 Sam. 17:45, 47). David's seemingly insignificant sling and stone prevailed, even to the extent of eventually reducing the Philistines to vassalage (2 Sam. 8), because (the commentaries explain) his enemy had been cut by its own sword. In other words, the defiant Philistines had defeated themselves.

At this point some commentaries cite another scriptural text, David's prophecy concerning the adversaries of his people: "they shall make their own tongue to fall upon themselves: all that see them shall flee away. / And all men shall fear, and shall declare the work of God" (Ps. 64:8-9). Concerning this passage, commentaries such as Matthew Henry's correlate tongue-shaped swords and sword-shaped tongues. In both 1 Samuel 17 and Wheatley's paraphrase of it, Goliath's pride informs and correlates his verbal defiance and his physical prowess. So in turn, swordless David's retort, expressing the swordlike word of God, is objectified in his flung "pebble" (Mason 1989, 65).

In short, words are weapons. Ministers likely emphasized this point, together with a specific application found in the commentaries: for people like David, who come swordless but in the name of God, the chief implement of victory is their adversaries' own language turned against them. This interpretation evidently under- lies Wheatley's enhanced depiction of the military victory of David, her surrogate in a verse paraphrase concerning the issue of servi- tude. Wheatley's performance in the paraphrase suggests that some- times her double-edged language, inspired by Scripture, cuts in two directions.

One direction of her poem is authorized: its meditation on an Old Testament type who adumbrates Christ's and the Christian church's victory over all Philistine-like forces. The other intimated direction of her poem is unauthorized: its meditation on a biblical hero as a surrogate for the slave poet who wishes likewise to emerge from personal servitude and to witness the release of her people from bondage. This sense, to be sure, is only implied, a nuance in Wheatley's paraphrase. But the internal concern with slavery in the biblical episode, read in light of the poet's insistence elsewhere (as we saw) that slavery defies providential intention, urges our sensi- tivity to such possible ambiguity in the paraphrase. Like David according to conventional eighteenth-century Protestant commen- taries on the Goliath episode, the poet apparently allows the famil- iar and comforting swordlike language of Scripture to reverse-cut, to condemn by "their own tongue," those Philistine-like Christians who enslave others.

This implied inversion is Wheatley's equivalent to David's retort to Goliath. While seeming to do little more than paraphrase and reinforce her Christian peers' traditional understanding of David, Wheatley's revised presentation of the Samuel passage also poten- tially suggests that Christian slavers are like the God-defying Phi- listines. With ruddy David (the Christic type) as her model, Wheatley comes swordless but armed with the swordlike Word of God conveyed through the small stone that is her poem. Her poem subtly reenacts the David and Goliath episode, as prevalently un- derstood in her time, to suggest that Philistine-like enslavers dis- guised as Christians "shall make their own tongue to fall upon themselves." The implied two-edged ambiguity of Wheatley's paraphrase converts the encounter between David and Goliath into a likely site of logonomic conflict, a place of friction between official and unlicensed applications of scriptural authority.

"Isaiah LXIII. 1-8"

Wheatley's Isaiah paraphrase similarly converts a standard comforting scriptural interpretation of her day into an indictment of certain Christians. In fact, Isaiah 63:1-8 shares several features with 1 Samuel 17. Both concern military incidents. In the Isaiah passage, which is a prophetic vision, a solitary warrior approaches Israel after a bloody encounter in Edom. This warrior threatens to "tread" on and "trample" all of the enemies of his people, and promises mercy only to those who are faithful to the Lord. Like solitary David in his encounter with Goliath, this envisioned savior in the Isaiah passage is identified by ruddiness, albeit in this instance his coloration is the result of the "blood" of the Edomites "sprinkled" upon him and his "red apparel." A previous defeat of the Edomites, it is worth noting, was the particular occasion of David's attainment of reputation (2 Sam. 8:13-14), a detail recalled by Isaiah. Both passages, linked in reference to David, are generally understood by Christians to foreshadow the New Testament victory of Christ over the dire effects of the Fall in Eden.

To appreciate Wheatley's version of Isaiah 63, it is important to consider the context of the prophet's prediction. Recalling David's victory, Isaiah prophesies the later appearance of a related savior, a prognostication intended to give heart to his people during their Babylonian captivity. Just as David's encounter with Goliath in the Samuel passage curtailed his servitude to Saul and prevented the enslavement of his people by the Philistines, Isaiah's vision foretells the coming of a David-like figure who will release the Israelites from their captivity. Representative commentaries on this prophecy, in fact, direct the reader to a line from one of David's verses, "the Lord turned again the captivity of Zion" (Ps. 126:1), and these commentaries speak of a day fixed for divine vengeance that must be awaited patiently. Isaiah's promise of "man's release," as Wheatley phrases it (Mason 1989, 75), doubtless appealed to the poet both as a slave and as a Christian.

This point in the third stanza of her poem actually demarcates the end of Wheatley's paraphrase. What follows in the remaining three stanzas is not based on verses 1-8 or, for that matter, on any subsequent verses in Isaiah 63. Similar to her management of the Samuel paraphrase, Wheatley now presents a dramatized scene of the savior's liberating battle against Goliath-like "haughty foes": "Beneath his feet the prostrate troops were spread, / And round him lay the dying and the dead" (Mason 1989, 75). Perhaps the imagery here was prompted by David's standing upon the fallen body of Goliath (1 Sam. 17:51; Mason 1989, 65) or by Psalm 18:38: "I have wounded them that they were not able to rise: they are fallen under my feet." Whatever the source, if any, Wheatley's presentation of combat here is comparable to that in her Samuel paraphrase, but significantly her description in the later verse departs altogether from the text of Isaiah 63:1-8.

The embellished combat scene in her Samuel paraphrase, as we saw, conforms to the generic conventions of biblical paraphrase and at the same time intimates an unauthorized application of the official interpretation of this biblical episode. The unexpected combat scene in Wheatley's Isaiah paraphrase, again centered on the issue of bondage, likewise appears to be a site of logonomic conflict, another two-edged verbal sword. In terms of authorized meaning, the combat scene envisions "man's release," the spiritual emancipation of Christians as foreshadowed by the end of the Babylonian Captivity. Unauthorized is a latent secular implication in this scene, the hint that Christians who enslave are like the doomed Babylonians. Again Wheatley's manner suggests a reversal: in the Isaiah paraphrase, as in the Samuel paraphrase, Christians who enslave are not aligned with God's chosen people but with those who defy divine providence.

This combination of sanctioned spiritual and interpolated temporal readings seems to inform the final stanza of the Isaiah paraphrase:

> Against thy Zion though her foes may rage,
> And all their cunning, all their strength engage,
> Yet she serenely on thy bosom lies,
> Smiles at their arts, all their force defies.   [Mason 76]

The bosom image derives from Isaiah 40:11 and perhaps reflects the prophet's later forecast of Zion's comfort (Isa. 51:3). A reversal of present circumstances is also indicated by "defies," the final word in the poem. In both 1 Samuel 17 and its paraphrase, the word "defy" and its variants are specifically associated with Goliath. The paraphrase of Isaiah 63:1-8 ends by suggesting that the pious defiance of those embosomed by God inverts the impious defiance of their Goliath-like adversaries.

Wheatley's reference to cunning is also pertinent. It likely alludes to Ephesians 4:14: "That we henceforth be no more children . . . carried about with every wind of doctrine, by the sleight of men, and cunning craftiness, whereby they lie in wait to deceive." Possibly, too, the mention of cunning recalls the chief trait of Esau (Gen. 25:27), the man who sold his birthright and who was reputed to be the ancestor of the routed Edomites mentioned at the start of Wheatley's paraphrase (Hastings 1909, 203).

"Cunning," however, has another biblical analogue. In Exodus this word describes the artistic rendering of divine inspiration in "all manner of work, of the engraver, and of the cunning workman" (35:35; cf. 36:8). This sense of special skill and knowledge is not the meaning of the word "cunning" as applied to Zion's foes, who are impiously devious. But if the Isaiah paraphrase (like the Samuel paraphrase) hints at reversals, including the Davidic refunding of defiance in response to Goliath-like forces, then we might reasonably entertain the possibility that Wheatley saw her artistic cunning as a pious antidote for the perverse cunning of those who use Scripture to justify the bondage of her race. Possibly she saw her cunning as divinely sanctioned, scripturally influenced or inspired. She apparently believed that her use of Holy Writ was doubly authorized by both select biblical commentaries and the ministerial practice of mingling religion and politics, two sources she encountered in the pew, discussion groups, and books. And from her point of view, this higher cunning would legitimate her pious use of deceptive appearance, her devious use of apparently conventional paraphrase, to implicate Christian slavers as latter-day Philistines and Babylonians. Wheatley would thereby redeem the "arts," invert the stratagems of deception mentioned in the last line of her poem, by means of a cunning art subserviently adhering to scriptural exegesis while also "defiantly" inferring an unorthodox temporal application.

Both paraphrases suggest a connection between divine justice and social justice, specifically spiritual redemption and social freedom. In forging this connection, Wheatley apparently manages her biblically influenced art as a verbal double-edged sword. She prophetically reminds her readers that the tongue of God's enemies—including Philistine-like and Babylonian-like Christians who enslave—will fatally "fall upon themselves." The clergy of her day put the Bible to political use, but their practice did not license the laity, much less a female slave, to make free with Scripture, the paradigmatic double-edged sword. In a significant sense, then, Wheatley arrogates ministerial privilege when she extrapolates an innovative secular message, even if only an intimated admonition, from the scriptural texts prompting her two paraphrases.

"On Being Brought from Africa to America"

The implications of Wheatley's surprising manner in these two paraphrases are best assessed in "On Being Brought from Africa to America." This poem has been read as the poet's repudiation of her African pagan heritage but not necessarily of her African racial identity (e.g., Isani 1979, 65). Derived from the surface of Wheatley's work, this appropriate reading has generally been sensitive to her political message and, at the same time, critically negligent concerning her artistic embodiment of this message in the language and execution of her poem. In this verse, however, Wheatley has adeptly managed biblical allusions that do more than serve as conventional authorizations for her writing. In her poem, these allusions also become logonomic sites where this legitimation is transformed to include an unlicensed artistry that in effect becomes exemplarily self-authorized. "On Being Brought from Africa to America" is very brief:

> 'Twas mercy brought me from my *Pagan* land,
> Taught my benighted soul to understand
> That there's a God, that there's a *Saviour* too:
> Once I redemption neither sought nor knew.
> Some view our sable race with scornful eye,
> "Their colour is a diabolic die."
> Remember, *Christians, Negros,* black as *Cain,*
> May be refin'd, and join th' angelic train. [Mason 1989, 53]

In this poem Wheatley finds various ways to defeat assertions alleging distinctions between the black and the white races (O'Neale 1986). She does more here than remark that representatives of the black race may be refined into angelic condition—purified or, as it were, made spiritually "white" through Christian redemption. She also indicates, apropos her point about spiritual change, that the Christian sense of Original Sin applies equally to both races. Both races inherit the barbaric spiritual blackness of sin (Jamison 1974, 413).

Particularly apt is the clever syntax of the last two lines of the poem: "Remember, *Christians, Negros,* black as *Cain,* / May be refin'd." These lines can be read to say that Christians—Wheatley uses the term *Christians* to refer to the white race—should remember that the black race is also a potential recipient of spiritual refinement; but these same lines can also be read to suggest that Christians should remember that in a spiritual sense white and black people are both the sin-darkened descendants of Canaan.

The poem, of course, refers to Cain. Although the association of Africans and the descendants of Cain was a prevalent motif during the eighteenth century, it is peculiar. Cain was the son of Adam and Eve who slew his brother and was subsequently marked on his forehead by God. But as Wheatley's African-British contemporary Ottobah Cugoano perspicaciously indicated in his autobiographical *Thoughts and Sentiments on the Evil of Slavery* (1787), there is no support for interpreting the mark on Cain as blackness of skin, nor (so it was generally thought) did any of Cain's descendants survive Noah's flood. (The possibility that the flood might not have destroyed everyone outside of Noah's ark was suggested by a few of the Church Fathers but was not a well-known or influential speculation.) In terms of the usual eighteenth-century Christian understanding of Noah's flood, in short, Cain could not be the ancestor of the black race.

In Wheatley's poem, as in other related eighteenth-century documents associating Adam's first son and the black race, "Cain" appears to be an oral corruption of "Canaan." Canaan was cursed by Noah to be "a servant of servants" (Gen. 9:25) in retaliation for his father Ham's filial disrespect. (There are many instances of such oral corruption, including in our day the post-1942 oral substitution of "to have a beef with" [meaning "complaint"] for the formal expression "to carry a brief for.") Although the corruption of the name "Canaan" is not unique to Wheatley, the merging of two biblical names and stories pertaining to curses in her poem conveys a secondary nuance that indeed recalls Cain's violence against his brother.

At this point in the poem, then, Wheatley secondarily alludes to Cain to suggest a spiritual brotherhood (as opposed to the perverted secular relationship) between the white and the black races, and primarily to Canaan to suggest the mutual spiritual inheritance of both sin-darkened races. In this way, Wheatley quietly revises the notion, held by many of her contemporaries (Wood 1990, 84-95) as heirs of centuries of unstable interpretations of Noah's progeny (Braude 1997), that Canaan was the progenitor of the black race, cursed by Noah (in God's stead, according to Christian apologists) to be slaves. At a spiritual level far surpassing the natural world, in Wheatley's view, both races are mutually reduced to servitude in a postlapsarian world where they are equally cursed.

Wheatley's revision of this myth concerning Canaan and the black race possibly emerges in part through her indicative use of italics (Levernier 1981), which equates Christians, Negroes, and Cain (Canaan); it is even more likely that this revisionary sense emerges as a result of the positioning of the comma after the word "Negros." Albeit grammatically correct, this comma imparts a trace of syntactic ambiguity. Read as direct address, the line of verse urges the white race to remember that the black race is included in the providential plan of redemption. Read as a declarative statement with an elliptical "that," Christians and Negroes are syntactically placed in grammatical apposition and spiritual equality. Wheatley's ambiguity here quietly instates both Christians and Negroes as the mutual offspring of Canaan—at least spiritually—who are both subject to refinement by divine grace.

In short, both races share a common heritage of Cainlike barbaric and criminal blackness, of Canaan-like "benighted soul," to which the poet refers in the second line of her poem. In spiritual terms, white and black people are jointly a "sable race," whose shared Adamic heritage is darkened by a "diabolic die," by the indelible stain of Original Sin. In this sense, white and black people are utterly equal before God, whose authority transcends the paltry earthly authorities who have argued for the inequality of the two races.

The poet needs some extrinsic warrant for making this point through the artistic maneuvers of her verse. This legitimation is implied in the last line of the poem, where Wheatley tells her readers to remember that sinners "May be refin'd and join th' angelic train." To instruct her readers to remember indicates that the poet is at this point (apparently) only deferring to a prior authority available to her outside of her own poem, an authority in fact licensing her poem. Specifically, Wheatley deftly manages two biblical allusions in her last line, both to Isaiah.

The first allusion occurs in the word "refin'd." Speaking for God, the prophet at one point says, "Behold, I have refined thee, but not with silver; I have chosen thee in the furnace of affliction" (Isa. 48:10). As placed in Wheatley's poem, this allusion can be read to say that being white (silver) is no sign of privilege (spiritually or culturally) because God's chosen are refined (purified, made spiritually white) through the charring afflictions that thusly blackened Christians and Negroes share in common as mutually benighted sinners. Wheatley may also cleverly suggest that the slaves' affliction includes their work in making dyes and in refining sugarcane (Levernier 1981), but in any event, her biblical allusion subtly validates her response to those individuals who attribute the notion of a "diabolic die" to Africans only. This allusion to Isaiah is an occasion of logonomic conflict, for here the poet at once accedes to and exceeds established authority in the artistic play on both the words and syntax that we have noted in her poem.

A second biblical allusion occurs in the word "train." Speaking of one of his visions, the prophet observes, "I saw also the Lord sitting upon a throne high and lifted up, and his train filled the temple" (Isa. 6:1). The Lord's attendant train is the retinue of the chosen referred to in the preceding allusion to Isaiah in Wheatley's poem. And, as we have seen, Wheatley claims that this angel-like following will be composed of those spiritual progeny of Canaan who have been refined, made spiritually bright and pure.

As the final word of this very brief poem, "train" is situated to draw more than average attention to itself. This word functions not only as a biblical allusion, but also as an echo of the opening two lines of the poem: "'Twas mercy brought me from my *Pagan* land, / Taught my benighted soul to understand." As the final word, "train" not only refers to the retinue of the divinely chosen but also to how these chosen are trained, "Taught . . . to understand." In circularly returning the reader to the beginning of the poem, this word transforms its biblical authorization into a form of unlicensed self-authorization. At this point of logonomic conflict, the poem combines biblical legitimation and the poet's sense of its achievement as inherent testimony to its argument. In effect, the reader is invited to return to the start of the poem and judge whether, on the basis of the work itself, the poet has proved her point about the equality of the two races in the matter of *cultural* as well as spiritual refinement.

Wheatley's management of the concept of refinement is doubly nuanced in her poem. The refinement that the poet invites the reader to assess is not only the one referred to by Isaiah, a spiritual refinement through affliction. She also means here the aesthetic refinement that likewise (evidently in her opinion *at least*) may accompany spiritual refinement. Wheatley's verse generally reveals her conscious concern with poetic grace, particularly in terms of certain eighteenth-century models (Davis 1953; Scruggs 1981). Nevertheless, when she associates spiritual and aesthetic refinement, she also participates in an extensive tradition of religious poets, such as George Herbert and Edward Taylor, who fantasized about the correspondence between the spiritual reconstruction of their souls and the aesthetic grace of their poetry. Like many Christian poets before her, Wheatley's poem also conducts its religious argument through its aesthetic attainment. As Wheatley pertinently wrote in "On Imagination" (1773), which similarly commingles religious and aesthetic refinements, she aimed to embody "blooming graces" in the "triumph of [her] song" (Mason 1989, 78).

Furthermore, Wheatley's use of the expression "angelic train" probably refers to more than the divinely redeemed, the saints who are biblically identified as celestial bodies, especially stars (Dan. 12:13). Her final biblical allusion to Isaiah in the poem also may echo a long history of poetic usage of similar language, exemplified in Milton's identification of the "gems of heaven" as the night's "starry train" (*Paradise Lost* 4:646). If Wheatley's image of "angelic train" participates in the heritage of such poetic discourse, then it too suggests her integration of aesthetic authority and biblical authority at this final moment of her verse.

Among her tests for aesthetic refinement, Wheatley doubtless had in mind her careful management of metrics and rhyme in "On Being Brought from Africa to America." Surely, too, she must have had in mind the clever use of syntax in the penultimate line of her poem, as well as her overall argument (conducted by means of imagery and nuance) concerning the equality of both races in terms of their mutually "benighted soul[s]." And she must have had in mind her subtle use of biblical allusions, which also may contain aesthetic allusions. The two allusions to Isaiah, in particular, initially serve to authorize her poem; then, in their circular reflexivity apropos the poem itself, they metamorphose into a form of the poet's self-authorization.

If the "angelic train" of her song actually enacts or performs her argument—that an African American woman can be trained, taught to understand, the refinements of religion and art—it carries a still more subtle suggestion of self-authorization. In this poem Wheatley gives her white audience polemical and artistic proof; and she gives her black audience an example of how to appropriate biblical ground to empower their related development of religious and cultural refinement. That there was an audience for her work is beyond question; the white response to her poetry was mixed (Robinson 1984, 39-46), and certain black responses were dramatic (Huddleston 1971; Jamison 1974). In appealing to these two audiences, Wheatley's persona assumes a dogmatic ministerial voice.

This voice is an important feature of her poem. In alluding to two verses from Isaiah, Wheatley intimates certain racial implications that are hardly conventional interpretations of these passages. The liberty she takes here surpasses the nuances embedded within either of her verse paraphrases of Scripture. In "On Being Brought from Africa to America" Wheatley alludes twice to Isaiah to refute stereotypical readings of skin color; she interprets these passages to refer to the spiritual benightedness shared in common by both races, diabolically dyed by sin. In thusly alluding to Isaiah, Wheatley initially seems to defer to scriptural authority in her observations, then transforms this legitimation into a form of artistic self-empowerment, and finally appropriates this biblical authority through the assumption of an interpreting ministerial voice.

When we consider how Wheatley manages these biblical allusions, particularly how she interprets them, we witness the extent to which she has become self-authorizing as a result of her training and refinement. Perhaps her sense of self in this instance demonstrates the degree to which she took to heart Enlightenment theories concerning personal liberty as an innate human right; these theories were especially linked to the abolitionist arguments advanced by the New England clergy with whom she had contact (Levernier 1991). Nevertheless, that an eighteenth-century colonial American woman (who was not a Quaker) should take on this traditionally male role is one surprise of Wheatley's poem. That this self-validating woman was a very young black slave makes this confiscation of ministerial role even more singular. Either of these implications would have profoundly disturbed the members of the Old South Congregational Church in Boston, had they detected her "ministerial" appropriation of the authority of Scripture.

Wheatley's persona in "On Being Brought from Africa to America" challenges the critical complaints that her poetry is imitative, inadequate, and unmilitant; her persona resists the conclusion that her poetry shows a resort to Scripture in lieu of imagination (Ogude 1981); and her persona suggests that her religious poetry can indeed be compatible with her political writings. In this regard, one might pertinently note that Wheatley's voice in this poem anticipates the ministerial role unwittingly assumed by an African American woman in the twenty-third chapter of Harriet Beecher Stowe's *The Minister's Wooing* (1859), in which Candace's hortatory words intrinsically reveal what male ministers have failed to teach about life and love.

In these ways, then, the biblical and aesthetic subtleties of Wheatley's poem advance her nuanced argument about refinement. Her argument in this instance recalls the earliest known plea for freedom (1723) by a slave, who likewise associates religion and literacy as the foreground for his emancipation (Ingersoll 1994, 779). In the course of her art, Wheatley demonstrates that she is no barbarian from a "*Pagan* land" who raises Cain (in the double sense of transgressing God and humanity). Her biblically authorized claim that the offspring of Canaan, marked like Cain, "may be refin'd" to "join th' angelic train" transmutes into her self-authorized artistry, in which her desire to raise Cain about the prejudices against her race is refined into the ministerial "angelic train" (the biblical and artistic train of thought) of her poem. This poetic demonstration of refinement, of "blooming graces" in both a spiritual and a cultural sense, is the "triumph in [her] song" entitled "On Being Brought from Africa to America."

If biblical allusions provided Wheatley with opportunities for creatively managing logonomic conflict, so did features of neoclassical tradition, the other major authority that influenced her verse (Sistrunk 1982). Devalued and subservient Fancy in "On Imagination," for example, serves as a trope for suppressed African American sentiment. Rather than align herself with Imagination as a means of escape from the world in this poem (Flanzbaum 1993, 78), the poet identifies with marginalized Fancy, which significantly is given the final word in this poem. It is Fancy which subtly instates love as the repressed natural bond that resists inhumane bondage, including the suppression of human feelings by Anglo-American neoclassical culture (McKay and Scheick 1994).

Unlike the other women featured in this book, Wheatley lived to see the start and end of the Revolutionary War, the chronological terminus of my discussion. The vast changes in economics and literacy that would have such a positive impact on post-Revolutionary female authors do not account for Wheatley's calculated use of logonomic conflict in her verse. Her experience of servitude, the thralldom that was the implied underside of the deep appreciation of freedom she reported in her poem to the Earl of Dartmouth, seems to have been the true catalyst of her engagement with this mode of artistic fashioning. Her keen sensitivity to freedom derived from her experience as a slave and found expression in a related nexus of mutually constitutive opposition: a subtle unlicensed ministerial (prophetic) application of Scripture presented sotto voce in the midst of an endorsement of the authorized (standard) reading of a biblical passage.

Although Wheatley employs logonomic conflict as a deliberate aesthetic device in her verse, her artistry is not free from the social anxieties that seismically disrupt the writings of Anne Bradstreet, Mary English, Elizabeth Hanson, Elizabeth Ashbridge, and Esther Edwards Burr. Wheatley may deftly manage what these women only unwittingly express, but the tug-of-war over authority registered in her use of biblical allusion is as much an underground performance as was theirs. Wheatley's social position as a young slave girl, her personal experience so antithetical to her expressed love of freedom, is inadvertently represented in the subjugation of her sotto voce resistant aesthetics below the surface of her outward acquiescence to conventional authorization. Her sentiment, in short, tends finally to be as veiled from the reader as are the subterranean feelings of earlier colonial women authors.

Wheatley's management of logonomic conflict, therefore, might be vulnerable to the observation that she failed to assess the constraint on her writing exerted by her inequality of power within her acquired culture (Burke 1991, 33, 38). However ingenious or subversive her artistry, the argument might continue, Wheatley failed to recognize that the positioning of her sentiment beneath the surface of the conventional was less an act of resistance than a reenactment of the slave's daily experience of oppression. And, the argument against her might conclude, even if this issue of power relations were overlooked, could Wheatley's particular stratagem ever have accomplished much in changing the social views of her times? (This question, one may note incidentally, must then perhaps also be applied more broadly to minority literature, which tends to embed political resistance within tropes [Slemon 1990, 31]). There is no evidence, for instance, that Wheatley's contemporaries detected her symbolic appropriations; and given her social position there is reason to doubt that she meant them to be specifically detected, at least consciously. And the skeptic may raise an eyebrow to the suggestion that possibly Wheatley meant her artistic manner to insinuate her revisionary message within the recesses of her reader's mind, where her design would go undetected as such but where in the long run it might prove effective in changing thought. Nor would this doubter, I am sure, approve of the possible explanation that Wheatley simply enjoyed the cunning craft of covertly transforming her personal subjection as object into an emancipated prophetic presence as subject.

In Wheatley's case I cannot definitively counter the skeptic. One's way of reading and assessing her work, like any other literary production, depends on one's perspective and values. But I will venture the thought that maybe we expect too much if we insist that Wheatley conform to the current agendas for and readings of the social text of our time. Whether we see her finally as resistant to or as complicit in the social text of her day, Wheatley surely deserves our appreciation at least for the wonder of her performance, which is special and different even within the restricted context of writings by women in northeastern colonial America.

As I have suggested in this chapter, it is the piously "defiant" and "cunning" Wheatley, as seen in her verse management of Scripture, who deserves more appreciation as a social critic and as an artist. Embedded within her surface compliance with authorized biblical and poetic traditions is a second voice. By being second, this voice may in some sense remain in bondage to the more dominant voice of communal authority, but it does indeed speak. Empowered by the swordlike Word of God and encroaching upon ministerial privilege, this swordless voice turns the language of Christian enslavers against themselves as she announces an unconventional message in a manner that crosses gender and social boundaries. To hear this restrained, if subtly defiant, voice is to enrich specifically our appreciation of Wheatley's art and generally our estimation of the range of northeastern colonial American women's expression of logonomic conflict.

Conclusion

There is an episode, designed to be humorous, in the first missive of J. Hector St. John de Crèvecoeur's *Letters from an American Farmer* (1782) that bears a parenthetical relationship to the foregoing discussion of my book. The fictional narrator of this and the following eleven letters reports his wife's vehement opposition to his epistolary undertaking, which leads to a consultation with a minister concerning the propriety of such activity. At first, his wife tries to dissuade her husband by emphasizing the shame and embarrassment he should properly feel, given his primitive colonial condition, in writing in a culturally impoverished manner to someone of learning and taste. After the minister scrupulously approves of the enterprise, however, the author's wife changes tack and now warns her husband of the risk to his local reputation. She predicts that their neighbors, after learning of these letters, will accuse him of idleness and vain notions. "For God's sake let it be kept a profound secret among us," she desperately pleads, "let it be as great a secret as if it was some heinous crime" (47-48).

For the most part, the letter is satiric in manner, its point being (as reinforced by the very title of Crèvecoeur's book) that leisure and artistic writing in the American settlements will shed their aristocratic status and eventually become egalitarian activities. "The art of writing is just like unto every other art of man," the narrator reiterates in a reliable moment in his account. "It is acquired by habit and by perseverance" (45). In other words, writing for pleasure—the evidence of culture—will emerge naturally as a property of the burgeoning new American Republic.

Whether or not Crèvecoeur's document accurately suggests that late colonial men associated types of writing with social rank, it is significant (apropos the focus of my study) that the reformist satire on class differences in this letter is rendered through a conformist satire on gender differences. That is to say, the narrator's wife bears the brunt of the humor of this missive. It is she, not the author or the minister or the gentleman, who gets implicitly trammeled in ridicule when, for typical example, she ingenuously contends that her farmer husband should "be ashamed to write unto a man who has never in his life done a single day's work" (41) and that her spouse should imitate his father, as "one of *yea* and *nay*, of few words" (48). It is she, not her husband or the clergyman or the aristocrat, who is naively preoccupied with class concerns and who, in effect, desires to conserve her inferior place in the social order. It is she, not the three men, who reacts to the province of writing for pleasure as if it were, in her phrase, "some heinous crime." As portrayed in the letter, the wife conforms to women's long-standing lot as secondary in relation to men, all three of whom are represented in the letter as intrinsically more sophisticated than she. And, most pertinent to the subject of my book, the wife exhibits a full-blown variety, if a parodic hybrid, of the anxiety toward writing that often exerted an underground pressure in the literary compositions of colonial American women.

As Crèvecoeur's depiction of the farmer's wife indicates, the traditional social construction of women as intellectually, socially, and culturally inferior to men had not significantly altered by the eve of the signing of the Treaty of Paris in 1783. Nor would bivocalism, ellipsis, disjunction, bifurcation, resistance, subversion, and ambiguity—the subtle, usually subterranean features of colonial American women writers' literary expressions of personal identity—vanish from the early republican female writings in the offing. Such future indications of logonomic conflict would emerge in American women's postcolonial writings despite the fact that their cultural situation was slowly improving.

The formation of subscription and circulation libraries, the emergence of open defenses of female education, and other related post-

Revolutionary economic and ideological developments would foster the spread of literacy and authorship among women. In the early Republic, in fact, female authored works would become prominent, many featuring an interest in history (Baym 1995, 1992). Fiction, however, would become a foremost genre of choice for women.

It is difficult to determine who primarily read the fiction written by early national women. The novels themselves most frequently implied white, literate, unmarried young women as their principal readers. Women were also the putative victims of the genre. Although signatures in extant copies of some of these works suggest that there were a number of novels avidly read by both women and men (Davidson 1986, 75-77), women were likely the main consumers of this fiction. Women conversed with one another about novels at social gatherings and in letters. They also exchanged copies of these books and read aloud from them in each other's presence. Women, who as a group had lagged behind men in literacy for centuries, doubtless enhanced their reading and writing skills, not to mention their general knowledge, by reading novels. Through the turn of the eighteenth century, moreover, these books nurtured in women and men alike an egalitarian sense of self-worth that merged with the rise of national identity in post-Revolutionary America.

By the close of the eighteenth century, the genre of fiction had already acquired a heritage of suspicion. In one or another way, fiction was thought of as a stimulator of the imagination, that deceiving "feminine" faculty of the mind so reviled by the defenders of "masculine" reason. In response to this heritage, the early American novel customarily protested its own innocence and, whatever the truth of the matter, insisted on its difference from the pernicious fiction said to ruin young women. It was this potentially subversive genre that early national female authors proclaimed to reform, to put to proper educational and historical use.

Apparently, however, the polymorphous nature of the genre made fiction a very attractive medium to these women for other unacknowledged reasons. The genre accommodated the equivocal expression of female interrogations of cultural authority far more flexibly than did the literary modes explored in the preceding chapters of this book. The Bakhtinian heteroglossia characteristic of the novel could readily engage and disguise a panoply of attitudes ranging from presentation of antithetical social possibilities entertained simultaneously without resolution to the suggestion of potentially culturally transgressive subtextual insinuations.

Such a pattern seems to be true, for example, for Susanna Haswell Rowson's *Charlotte Temple* (English ed. 1791; American ed. 1794), the most widely read if not the most original of early national novels written by women. This work was commonly perceived in its day and later as a morality tale, but (as recent critical studies have shown) the sincerity, or at least the efficacy, of Rowson's prefatory insistence that she fashioned her novel to warn "the thoughtless of the fair sex" about their "morals and conduct" (xlix-l) is open to question. Although novelists like Rowson speak in this way to legitimize writing in a disreputable genre, their usually brief messages about female virtue seem frail in comparison to the prolonged, often sensationalistic drama of their ingénue's downfall or close encounters with ruin. Moreover, specific plot elements associating fallen women with the values of republican national identity—independence, personal expression, and rebellion against authority—occasionally appear to overpower an author's expressed moralistic admonitions concerning the propriety of female dependence, self-denial, and silent submission (Davidson 1986). Female-authored late-eighteenth-century novels, in short, frequently adapt the older colonial valuation of marriage and family order to the perceived needs of the new Republic; but these same works (sometimes by accident, sometimes by design) often imply problems with patriarchal authority and female inequality in the young nation celebrating independence as a virtue.

Although the ability to form and articulate a sense of personal identity improved somewhat for female authors during and after the Revolution, opportunities to do so were far from ideal (Kerber 1980). It is not surprising, then, that logonomic conflict was a feature of their republican literary productions, especially fiction. The literary loci of ideological dissonance, the textual sites where women anxiously negotiated between official and personal authority, changed during the early national years. But these later instances were nonetheless kindred to an earlier variety: scarcely noticeable seismic tensions below the apparently conventional surface of writings by various colonial American female authors, who in uncomfortable textual moments expressed their otherwise repressed personal responses to theocratic authority.

Works Cited

Akers, Charles W. 1975. "'Our Modern Egyptians': Phillis Wheatley and the Whig Campaign against Slavery in Revolutionary Boston." *Journal of Negro History* 60:399-410.

Andrews, William D. 1970. "The Printed Funeral Sermons of Cotton Mather." *Early American Literature* 5:24-44.

Bailyn, Bernard. 1960. *The Forming of American Society: Needs and Opportunities for Study.* Chapel Hill: Univ. of North Carolina Press.

Baker, Houston A., Jr. 1991. *Workings of the Spirit: The Poetics of Afro-American Women's Writing.* Chicago: Univ. of Chicago Press.

Ball, Kenneth R. 1973. "Puritan Humility in Anne Bradstreet's Poetry." *Cithara* 13:29-41.

Baym, Nina. 1995. *American Women Writers and the Work of History, 1790-1860.* New Brunswick, N.J.: Rutgers Univ. Press.

———. 1992. *Feminism and American Literary History.* New Brunswick, N.J.: Rutgers Univ. Press.

———, et al. 1994. *The Norton Anthology of American Literature: Fourth Edition, Volume 1.* New York: Norton.

Berkin, Carol. 1996. *First Generations: Women in Colonial America.* New York: Hill and Wang.

Berry, Philippa. 1989. *Of Chastity and Power: Elizabethan Literature and the Unmarried Queen.* London: Routledge.

Bosco, Ronald A., ed. 1989. *The Poems of Michael Wigglesworth.* Lanham, Md.: Univ. Press of America.

Bowden, John. 1850-54. *The History of the Society of Friends in America.* 2 vols. London: W. and F.G. Cash.

Bowers, Bathsheba. 1709. *An Alarm Sounded to Prepare the Inhabitants of the World to Meet the Lord in the Way of His Judgment.* New York: [publisher uncertain].

Boyarin, Daniel. 1993. "Paul and the Genealogy of Gender." *Representations* 41:1-33.

Boyer, Paul, and Stephen Nissenbaum. 1974. *Salem Possessed: The Social Origins of Witchcraft.* Cambridge: Harvard Univ. Press.
————, eds. 1977. *The Salem Witchcraft Papers.* New York: Da Capo Press.
Braude, Benjamin. 1997. "The Sons of Noah and the Construction of Ethnic and Geographical Identities in the Medieval and Early Modern Periods." *William and Mary Quarterly* 54:103-42.
Breen, T.H. 1993. "Narrative of Commercial Life: Consumption, Ideology, and Community on the Eve of the American Revolution." *William and Mary Quarterly* 50:471-501.
Breitwieser, Mitchell Robert. 1990. *American Puritanism and the Defense of Mourning: Religion, Grief, and Ethnology in Mary White Rowlandson's Captivity Narrative.* Madison: Univ. of Wisconsin Press.
Brewster, Martha. 1758. *Poems on Divers Subjects.* Boston: Edes and Gill.
Brooke, Frances. [1769] 1961. *The History of Emily Montague.* Toronto: Mc-Clelland and Stewart.
Brown, Kathleen M. 1996. *Good Wives, Nasty Wenches, and Anxious Patriarchs: Gender, Race, and Power in Colonial Virginia.* Chapel Hill: Univ. of North Carolina Press.
Brown, William Hill. [1789] 1961. *The Power of Sympathy.* Ed. Herbert Brown. Boston: New Frontiers Press.
Bruce, Philip Alexander. 1910. *Institutional History of Virginia in the Seventeenth Century.* 2 vols. New York: Putnam's Sons.
Burke, Helen M. 1991. "The Rhetoric and Politics of Marginality: The Subject of Phillis Wheatley." *Tulsa Studies in Women 's Literature* 10:31-45.
Burroughs, Margaret G. 1974. "Do Birds of a Feather Flock Together?" *Jackson State Review* 6, 1:61-73.
Calder, Isabel M., ed. 1935. *Colonial Captivities, Marches and Journeys.* New York: Macmillan.
Caldwell, Patricia. 1988. "Why Our First Poet Was a Woman: Bradstreet and the Birth of an American Poetic Voice." *Prospects* 13:1-35.
Carr, Lois Green, and Lorena S. Walsh. 1979. "The Planter's Wife: The Experience of White Women in Seventeenth-Century Maryland." In *A Heritage of Her Own: Toward a New Social History of American Women,* ed. Nancy F. Cott and Elizabeth H. Pleck, 25-57. New York: Simon and Schuster.
Cheever, George F. 1860. "Philip English—Part Second." *Historical Collections of the Essex Institute* 2:237-48.

————. 1859. "A Sketch of Philip English." *Historical Collections of the Essex Institute* 1:157-81.

Cole, David L. 1994. "Mistresses of the Household: Distaff Publishing in London, 1588-1700." *CEA Critic* 56, 2:20-30.

Collins, Terrence. 1975. "Phillis Wheatley: The Dark Side of the Poetry." *Phylon* 36, 1:78-88.

Colman, Benjamin. 1735. *Reliquiae Turellae, et Lachrymae Paternae.* (Bound with *Memoirs of the Life and Death of the Pious and Ingenious Mrs. Jane Turell* by Ebenezer Turell.) Boston: S. Kneeland and T. Green.

Cowell, Pattie. 1994. "Early New England Women Poets: Writing as Vocation." *Early American Literature* 29:103-21.

————, ed. 1981. *Women Poets in Pre-Revolutionary America, 1650-1775: An Anthology.* Troy, N.Y.: Whitston.

Cremin, Lawrence A. 1970. *American Education: The Colonial Experience, 1607-1783.* New York: Harper.

Crèvecoeur, J. Hector St. John de. [1782; 1925] 1981. Letters from an American Farmer *and* Sketches of Eighteenth-Century America. Ed. Albert E. Stone. Harmondsworth, England: Penguin Books.

Cudworth, Ralph. [1678] 1845. *The True Intellectual System of the Universe.* 3 vols. London: Thomas Tegg.

Cugoano, Ottobah. [1787] 1969. *Thoughts and Sentiments on the Evil of Slavery.* London: Dawsons of Pall Mall.

Daly, Robert. 1978. *God's Altar: The World and the Flesh in Puritan Poetry.* Berkeley: Univ. of California Press.

Davidson, Cathy N. 1986. *Revolution and the Word: The Rise of the Novel in America.* New York: Oxford Univ. Press.

Davidson, Edward H., and William J. Scheick. 1994. *Paine, Scripture, and Authority:* The Age of Reason *as Religious and Political Idea.* Bethlehem: Lehigh Univ. Press.

Davis, Arthur P. 1953. "The Personal Elements in the Poetry of Phillis Wheatley." *Phylon* 12, 2:191-98.

Davis, Natalie Zemon. 1995. *Women on the Margins: Three Seventeenth-Century Lives.* Cambridge: Harvard Univ. Press.

Davis, Richard Beale. 1978. *Intellectual Life in the Colonial South, 1585-1763.* 3 vols. Knoxville: Univ. of Tennessee Press.

Dayton, Cornelia Hughes. 1995. *Women before the Bar: Gender, Law, and Society in Connecticut, 1639-1789.* Chapel Hill: Univ. of North Carolina Press.

Derounian-Stodola, Kathryn Zabelle. 1990. "'The excellency of the inferior sex': The Commendatory Writings on Anne Bradstreet." *Studies in Puritan American Spirituality* 1:129-47.

Derounian-Stodola, Kathryn Zabelle, and James Arthur Levernier. 1993. *The Indian Captivity Narrative, 1550-1900.* New York: Twayne.

Douglas, Ann. 1977. *The Feminization of American Culture.* New York: Knopf.

Dudden, Faye E. 1994. *Women in the American Theatre: Actresses and Audiences, 1790-1870.* New Haven: Yale Univ. Press.

Eberwein, Jane Donahue. 1981. "'No rhet'ric we expect': Argumentation in Bradstreet's 'The Prologue.'" *Early American Literature* 16:19-26.

Edkins, Carol. 1980. "Quest for Community: Spiritual Autobiographies of Eighteenth-Century Quaker and Puritan Women in America." In *Women's Autobiography: Critical Essays,* ed. by Estelle C. Jelinek, 39-52. Bloomington: Univ. of Indiana Press.

Eldred, Janet Carey, and Peter Mortensen. 1993. "Gender and Writing Instruction in Early America: Lessons from Didactic Fiction." *Rhetoric Review* 12:25-53.

Ellison, Julie. 1984. "The Sociology of 'Holy Indifference': Sarah Edwards' Narrative." *American Literature* 56:479-95.

Erkkila, Betsy. 1993. "Phillis Wheatley and the Black American Revolution." In *A Mixed Race: Ethnicity in Early America,* ed. Frank Shuffelton, 225-40. New York: Oxford Univ. Press.

Felker, Christopher D. 1994. "'The Tongues of the learned are insufficient': Phillis Wheatly, Publishing Objectives, and Personal Liberty." *Resources for American Literary Study* 20:149-79.

Fichtelberg, Joseph. 1989. *The Complex Image: Faith and Method in American Autobiography.* Philadelphia: Univ. of Pennsylvania Press.

Findlen, Paula. 1995. "Translating the New Science: Women and the Circulation of Knowledge in Enlightenment Italy." *Configurations* 3:167-206.

Fiske, Sarah Symmes. 1704. *A Confession of Faith.* Boston: Benson Eliot.

Flanzbaum, Hilene. 1993. "Unprecedented Liberties: Re-Reading Phillis Wheatley." *MELUS* 18:71-81.

Foster, Frances Smith. 1993. *Written by Herself: Literary Production of African American Women, 1746-1892.* Bloomington: Indiana Univ. Press.

Foster, Stephen. 1991. *The Long Argument: English Puritanism and the Shaping of New England Culture, 1570-1700.* Williamsburg, Va.: Institute of Early American History and Culture.

Foucault, Michel. 1977. *Language, Counter-Memory, Practice: Selected Es-*

says and Interviews by Michel Foucault. Ed. Donald F. Bouchard. Ithaca: Cornell Univ. Press.

Foxe, John. [1563] 1965. *The Acts and Monuments of These Latter and Perilous Days.* Ed. Stephen Cattley and George Townsend. 8 vols. New York: AMS Press.

Frerichs, Ernest S., ed. 1988. *The Bible and Bibles in America.* Atlanta: Scholars Press.

Frost, William J. 1973. *The Quaker Family in Colonial America: A Portrait of the Society of Friends.* New York: St. Martin's Press.

Frye, Susan. 1993. *Elizabeth I: The Competition for Representation.* New York: Oxford Univ. Press.

Gallagher, Catherine. 1994. *Nobody's Story: The Vanishing Acts of Women Writers in the Marketplace, 1670-1820.* Berkeley: Univ. of California Press.

Gilman, Ernest B. 1986. *Iconoclasm and Poetry in the English Reformation: Down Went Dagon.* Chicago: Univ. of Chicago Press.

Godbeer, Richard. 1992. *The Devil's Dominion: Magic and Religion in Early New England.* Cambridge: Cambridge Univ. Press.

Goen, C.C., ed. 1972. *The Works of Jonathan Edwards, Volume 4: The Great Awakening.* New Haven: Yale Univ. Press.

Greenslade, S.L., ed. 1963. *The Cambridge History of the Bible.* 3 vols. Cambridge: Cambridge Univ. Press.

Hall, David D. 1989. *Worlds of Wonders, Days of Judgment: Popular Religious Belief in Early New England.* New York, Knopf.

Hamilton, Edith. 1940. *Mythology.* Boston: Little, Brown.

Hammond, Jeffrey A. 1993. *Sinful Self, Saintly Self: The Puritan Experience of Poetry.* Athens: Univ. of Georgia Press.

Harris, Sharon M. 1993. "Early American Women's Self-Creating Acts." *Resources for American Literary Study* 19:223-45.

———, ed. 1996. *American Women Writers to 1800.* New York: Oxford Univ. Press.

Hastings, James. 1909. *Dictionary of the Bible.* New York: Charles Scribner's Sons.

Hayes, Kevin J. 1996. *A Colonial Woman's Bookshelf.* Knoxville: Univ. of Tennessee Press.

Hobby, Elaine. 1988. *Virtue of Necessity: English Women's Writing, 1649-88.* Ann Arbor: Univ. of Michigan Press.

Hodge, Robert. 1990. *Literature as Discourse: Textual Strategies in English and History.* Baltimore: Johns Hopkins Univ. Press.

Hodge, Robert, and Gunther Kress. 1988. *Social Semiotics.* Ithaca: Cornell Univ. Press.

Holmes, Thomas J. 1940. *Cotton Mather: A Bibliography of His Works.* 2 vols. Cambridge: Harvard Univ. Press.

Holquist, Michael, ed. 1981. *The Dialogic Imagination: Four Essays by M. M. Bakhtin.* Austin: Univ. of Texas Press.

Horn, James. 1994. *Adapting to a New World: English Society in the Seventeenth-Century Chesapeake.* Chapel Hill: Univ. of North Carolina Press.

Hubbard, Dolan. 1994. *The Sermon and the African American Literary Imagination.* Columbia: Univ. of Missouri Press.

Hudak, Leona M. 1978. *Early American Women Printers and Publishers, 1639-1820.* Metuchen, N.J.: Scarecrow Press.

Huddleston, Eugene L. 1971. "Matilda's 'On Reading the Poems of Phillis Wheatley, the African Poetess.' " *Early American Literature* 5:57-67.

Hume, Sophia. 1747. *An Exhortation to the Inhabitants of the Province of South-Carolina.* Philadelphia: William Bradford.

Ingersoll, Thomas N. 1994. "'Releese us out of this Cruell Bondegg': An Appeal from Virginia in 1723." *William and Mary Quarterly* 51:777-82.

Isani, Mukhtar Ali. 1979. "'Gambia on My Soul': Africa and the African in the Writings of Phillis Wheatley." *MELUS* 6, 1:64-72.

———. 1982. "Phillis Wheatley and the Elegaic Mode." In *Critical Essays on Phillis Wheatley,* ed. William H. Robinson, 208-14. Boston: G.K. Hall.

Iser, Wolfgang. 1978. *The Act of Reading: A Theory of Aesthetic Response.* Baltimore: Johns Hopkins Univ. Press.

Jamison, Angelene. 1974. "Analysis of Selected Poetry of Phillis Wheatley." *Journal of Negro Education* 43, 3:408-16.

Kamensky, Jane. 1992. "Words, Witches, and Woman Trouble: Witchcraft, Disorderly Speech, and Gender Boundaries in New England." *Essex Institute Historical Collections* 128:286-307.

Karlsen, Carol F., and Laurie Crumpacker, eds. 1984. *The Journal of Esther Edwards Burr, 1754-1757.* New Haven: Yale Univ. Press.

Kelley, Mary. 1992. "'Vindicating the Equality of Female Intellect': Women and Authority in the Early Republic." *Prospects* 17:1-27.

Kendrick, Robert L. 1993. "Snatching a Laurel, Wearing a Mask: Phillis Wheatley's Literary Nationalism and the Problem of Style." *Style* 27:222-51.

Kenyon, Olga. 1992. *800 Years of Women's Letters.* Phoenix Mill, England: Alan Sutton.

Kerber, Linda K. 1980. *Women of the Republic: Intellect and Ideology in Revolutionary America.* Chapel Hill: Univ. of North Carolina Press.

Kern, Louis J. 1993. "Eros, the Devil, and the Cunning Woman: Sexuality and the Supernatural in European Antecedents and in the Seventeenth-Century Salem Witchcraft Cases." *Essex Institute Historical Collections* 129:3-38.

Kibbey, Ann. 1982. "Mutations of the Supernatural: Witchcraft, Remarkable Providences, and the Power of Puritan Men." *American Quarterly* 34:125-48.

Knapp, Jeffrey. 1993. "Preachers and Players in Shakespeare's England." *Representations* 44:29-59.

Knight, Denise D., ed. 1989. *Cotton Mather's Verse in English.* Newark: Univ. of Delaware Press.

Knight, Lucian Lamar, ed. 1910. *Biographical Dictionary.* Vol. 15 of *Library of Southern Literature,* ed. Edwin Anderson Alderman and Joel Chandler Harris. Atlanta: Martin and Hoyt Co.

Koehler, Lyle. 1980. *A Search for Power: The "Weaker Sex" in Seventeenth-Century New England.* Urbana: Univ. of Illinois Press.

Kristeva, Julia. 1980. *Desire in Language: A Semiotic Approach to Literature and Art.* Trans. Thomas Gora, Alice Jardin, and Leon Roudiez. New York: Columbia Univ. Press.

Lang, Amy Schrager. 1987. *Prophetic Women: Anne Hutchinson and the Problem of Dissent in the Literature of New England.* Berkeley and Los Angeles: Univ. of California Press.

Laughlin, Rosemary M. 1970. "Anne Bradstreet: Poet in Search of Form." *American Literature* 42:1-17.

Levernier, James A. 1991. "Phillis Wheatley and the New England Clergy." *Early American Literature* 26:21-38.

———. 1993. "Style as Protest in the Poetry of Phillis Wheatley." *Style* 27:172-93.

———. 1981. "Wheatley's 'On Being Brought from Africa to America.'" *Explicator* 40, 1:25-26.

Levernier, James A., and Douglas R. Wilmes, eds. 1983. *American Writers Before 1800.* 3 vols. Westport, Conn.: Greenwood Press.

Lewalski, Barbara Kiefer. 1993. *Writing Women in Jacobean England.* Cambridge: Harvard Univ. Press.

Lockridge, Kenneth A. 1974. *Literacy in Colonial New England.* New York: W.W. Norton.

Logan, Lisa. 1993. "Mary Rowlandson's Captivity and the 'Place' of the Female Subject." *Early American Literature* 28:255-77.

Logan, Martha. 1772. *A Treatise on Gardening*. Charleston: [publisher uncertain].

Luxon, Thomas H. 1995. *Literal Figures: Puritan Allegory and the Reformation Crisis in Representation*. Chicago: Univ. of Chicago Press.

Main, Gloria. 1991. "An Inquiry into When and Why Women Learned to Write in Colonial New England." *Journal of Social History* 24:579-89.

Margerum, Eileen. 1982. "Anne Bradstreet's Public Poetry and the Tradition of Humility." *Early American Literature* 17:152-60.

Marshall, David. 1993. "Writing Masters and 'Masculine Exercises' in *The Female Quixote*." *Eighteenth-Century Fiction* 5:105-35.

Martin, Wendy. 1979. "Anne Bradstreet's Poetry: A Study of Subversive Piety." In *Shakespeare's Sisters: Feminist Essays on Women Poets,* ed. Sandra M. Gilbert and Susan Gubar, 19-31. Bloomington: Indiana Univ. Press.

Mason, Julian D., Jr., ed. 1989. *The Poems of Phillis Wheatley.* Chapel Hill: Univ. of North Carolina Press.

Masson, Margaret W. 1976. "The Typology of the Female as a Model for the Regenerate: Puritan Preaching, 1690-1750." *Signs* 2:304-15.

Mather, Cotton. [1741] 1978. *Ornaments for the Daughters of Zion*. Intro. Pattie Cowell. Delmar, N.Y.: Scholar's Facsimiles and Reprints.

Matson, R. Lynn. 1982. "Phillis Wheatley—Soul Sister?" In *Critical Essays on Phillis Wheatley,* ed. William H. Robinson, 113-22. Boston: G.K. Hall.

Mawer, Randall R. 1980. "'Farewel Dear Babe': Bradstreet's Elegy for Elizabeth." *Early American Literature* 15:29-41.

McElrath, Joseph R., Jr., and Allan P. Robb, eds. 1981. *The Complete Works of Anne Bradstreet.* Boston: Twayne.

McKay, Michele, and William J. Scheick. 1994. "The Other Song in Phillis Wheatley's 'On Imagination.'" *Studies in the Literary Imagination* 27:71-84.

Meserve, Walter J. 1977. *An Emerging Entertainment: The Drama of the American People to 1828.* Bloomington: Univ. of Indiana Press.

Middlekauff, Robert. 1971. *The Mathers: Three Generations of Puritan Intellectuals, 1596-1728.* New York: Oxford Univ. Press.

Mignon, Charles W. 1968. "Edward Taylor's *Preparatory Meditations:* A Decorum of Imperfection." *Publications of the Modern Language Association* 83:1423-28.

Miller, J. Hillis. 1989. "The Function of Literary Theory at the Present

Time." In *The Future of Literary Theory,* ed. Ralph Cohen, 102-11. New York: Routledge.

Miller, Nancy K. 1986. "Changing the Subject: Authorship, Writing, and the Reader." In *Feminist Studies/Critical Studies,* ed. Teresa de Lauretis, 102-20. Bloomington: Indiana Univ. Press.

Monaghan, E. Jennifer. 1991. "Family Literacy in Early 18th-Century Boston: Cotton Mather and His Children." *Reading Research Quarterly* 26:342-70.

———. 1989. "Literacy Instruction and Gender in Colonial New England." In *Reading in America: Literature and Social History,* ed. Cathy N. Davidson, 53-80. Baltimore: Johns Hopkins Univ. Press.

Moran, Gerald R., and Maris A. Vinovskis. 1992. *Religion, Family, and the Life Course: Explorations in the Social History of Early America.* Ann Arbor: Univ. of Michigan Press.

Morgan, Edmund S. 1966. *The Puritan Family: Religion and Domestic Relations in Seventeenth-Century New England.* Rev. ed. New York: Harper and Row.

Mulford, Carla J., ed. 1995. *Only for the Eye of a Friend: The Poems of Annis Boudinot Stockton.* Charlottesville: Univ. Press of Virginia.

Newman, William R. 1994. *Gehennical Fire: The Lives of George Starkey, an American Alchemist in the Scientific Revolution.* Cambridge: Harvard Univ. Press.

Ogude, S.E. 1981. "Slavery in the African Imagination: A Critical Perspective." *World Literature Today* 55:21-25.

O'Neale, Sondra. 1986. "A Slave's Subtle War: Phillis Wheatley's Use of Biblical Myth and Symbol." *Early American Literature* 21:144-65.

Ong, Walter J. 1967. *In the Human Grain: Further Explorations of Contemporary Culture.* New York: Macmillan.

Otten, Charlotte F., ed. 1992. *English Women's Voices, 1540-1700.* Miami: Florida International Univ. Press.

Pettengill, Claire C. 1992. "Sisterhood in a Separate Sphere: Female Friendship in Hannah Webster Foster's *The Coquette* and *The Boarding School.*" *Early American Literature* 27:185-203.

Pinckney, Elise, ed. 1972. *The Letterbook of Eliza Lucas Pinckney, 1739-1762.* Chapel Hill: Univ. of North Carolina Press.

Porterfield, Amanda. 1992. *Female Piety in Puritan New England: The Emergence of Religious Humanism.* New York: Oxford Univ. Press.

———. 1980. *Female Spirituality in America from Sarah Edwards to Martha Graham.* Philadelphia: Temple Univ. Press.

Pratt, Mary Louise. 1992. *Imperial Eyes: Travel Writing and Transculturation.* London: Routledge.

Reid, J.K., ed. 1954. *Calvin: Theological Treatises.* Philadelphia: Westminster Press.

Richards, Phillip M. 1993. "Phillis Wheatley, Americanization, the Sublime, and the Romance of America." *Style* 27:194-221.

———. 1992. "Phillis Wheatley and Literary Americanization." *American Quarterly* 44:163-91.

Richmond, Merle A. 1974. *Bid the Vassal Soar: Interpretive Essays on the Life and Poetry of Phillis Wheatley and George Mason Horton.* Washington, D.C.: Howard Univ. Press.

———. 1982. "On 'The barter of her soul.'" In *Critical Essays on Phillis Wheatley,* ed. William H. Robinson, 123-27. Boston: G.K. Hall.

Robinson, William H., ed. 1982. *Critical Essays on Phillis Wheatley.* Boston: G.K. Hall.

———, ed. 1984. *Phillis Wheatley and Her Writings.* New York: Garland.

Rosenmeier, Rosamond. 1991. *Anne Bradstreet Revisited.* Boston, Twayne.

———. 1977. "Divine Translation: A Contribution to the Study of Anne Bradstreet's Method in the Marriage Poems." *Early American Literature* 12:121-35.

Rosenthal, Bernard. 1993. *Salem Story: Reading the Witch Trials of 1692.* Cambridge: Cambridge Univ. Press.

Rowson, Susanna Haswell. [1791; 1828] 1991. *Charlotte Temple* and *Lucy Temple.* Ed. Ann Douglas. London: Penguin Books.

Rubin, Louis D., Jr., et al., eds. 1985. *The History of Southern Literature.* Baton Rouge: Louisiana State Univ. Press.

Scheick, William J. 1992. *Design in Puritan American Literature.* Lexington: Univ. Press of Kentucky.

———. 1974. *The Will and the Word: The Poetry of Edward Taylor.* Athens: Univ. of Georgia Press.

———, ed. [1670; 1724] 1989. *Two Mather Biographies:* Life and Death *and* Parentator. Bethlehem, Pa.: Lehigh Univ. Press.

Schibanoff, Susan. 1994. "Botticelli's *Madonna del Magnificat:* Constructing the Woman Writer in Early Humanist Italy." *Publications of the Modern Language Association* 109:190-206.

Schweitzer, Ivy. 1988. "Anne Bradsreet Wrestles with the Renaissance." *Early American Literature* 23:291-312.

———. 1991. *The Work of Self-Representation: Lyric Poetry in Colonial New England.* Chapel Hill: Univ. of North Carolina Press.

Scruggs, Charles. 1981. "Phillis Wheatley and the Poetical Legacy of Eighteenth-Century England." *Studies in Eighteenth-Century Culture* 10:279-
95.

Sennett, Richard. 1980. *Authority.* New York: Knopf.

Sewel, William. 1800. *The History of the Rise, Increase, and Progress, of the
Christian People Called Quakers.* 2 vols. London: J. Phillips.

Shea, Daniel B., Jr. 1968. *Spiritual Autobiography in Early America.*
Princeton: Princeton Univ. Press.

————, ed. 1990. "Some Account of the Fore Part of the Life of Elizabeth Ashbridge." In *Journeys in New Worlds: Early American Women's
Narratives,* ed. by William L. Andrews et al., 117-80. Madison: Univ.
of Wisconsin Press.

Shields, John C. 1993. "Phillis Wheatley's Subversion of Classical
Stylistics." *Style* 27:252-70.

Silverman, Kenneth. 1984. *The Life and Times of Cotton Mather.* New York:
Harper and Row.

Sistrunk, Albertha. 1982. "The Influence of Alexander Pope on the Writing Style of Phillis Wheatley." In *Critical Essays on Phillis Wheatley,* ed.
William H. Robinson, 175-88. Boston: G.K. Hall.

Slemon, Stephen. 1990. "Unsettling the Empire: Resistance Theory for
the Second World." *World Literature Written in English* 28:30-41.

Smith, Theophus H. 1994. *Conjuring Culture: Biblical Formations of Black
America.* New York: Oxford Univ. Press.

Smolinski, Reiner, ed. 1995. *The Threefold Paradise of Cotton Mather: An
Edition of "Triparadisus."* Athens: Univ. of Georgia Press.

Smucker, Esther F. 1995. *Good Night, My Son.* Elverson, Pa.: Olde Spring-
field Shoppe.

Spruill, Julia Cherry. 1938. *Women's Life and Work in the Southern Colonies.* Chapel Hill: Univ. of North Carolina Press.

Stanford, Ann. 1966. "Anne Bradstreet: Dogmatist and Rebel." *New England Quarterly* 39:373-89.

————. 1974. *Anne Bradstreet: The Worldly Puritan.* New York: Burt
Franklin.

Stanford, Donald E., ed. 1960. *The Poems of Edward Taylor.* New Haven:
Yale Univ. Press.

Starkey, Marion L. 1949. *The Devil in Massachusetts: A Modern Inquiry
into the Salem Witch Trials.* New York: Knopf.

Staten, Henry. 1993. "How the Spirit (Almost) Became Flesh: Gospel of
John." *Representations* 41:34-57.

Sweet, Timothy. 1988. "Gender, Genre, and Subjectivity in Anne Bradstreet's Early Elegies." *Early American Literature* 23:152-74.

Thickstun, Margaret Olofson. 1988. *Fictions of the Feminine: Puritan Doctrine and the Representation of Women.* Ithaca: Cornell Univ. Press.

Tobin, Lad. 1990. "A Radically Different Voice: Gender and Language in the Trials of Anne Hutchinson." *Early American Literature* 25:253-70.

Toulouse, Teresa A. 1992. "'My Own Credit': Strategies of (E)Valuation in Mary Rowlandson's Captivity Narrative." *American Literature* 64:655-76.

Turell, Ebenezer. 1735. *Memoirs of the Life and Death of the Pious and Ingenious Mrs. Jane Turell.* (Bound with *Reliquiae Turellae, et Lachrymae Paternae* by Benjamin Colman.) Boston: S. Kneeland and T. Green.

Ulrich, Laurel Thatcher. 1982. *Good Wives: Image and Reality in the Lives of Women in Northern New England, 1650-1750.* New York: Knopf.

VanDerBeets, Richard. 1984. *The Indian Captivity Narrative.* Lanham, Md.: Univ. Press of America.

Vaughan, Alden T., and Edward W. Clark, eds. 1981. *Puritans among the Indians: Accounts of Captivity and Redemption, 1676-1724.* Cambridge: Harvard Univ. Press.

Vella, Michael W. 1993. "Theology, Genre, and Gender: The Precarious Place of Hannah Adams in American Literary History." *Early American Literature* 28:21-41.

Waller, Jennifer R. 1974. "'My Hand a Needle Better Fits': Anne Bradstreet and Women Poets in the Renaissance." *Dalhousie Review* 54:436-50.

Watson, Marsha. 1996. "A Classic Case: Phillis Wheatley and Her Poetry." *Early American Literature* 31:103-32.

Watson, Patricia Ann. 1991. *The Angelical Conjunction: The Preacher Physicians of Colonial New England.* Knoxville: Univ. of Tennessee Press.

Watts, Emily Stipes. 1977. *The Poetry of American Women from 1632 to 1945.* Austin: Univ. of Texas Press.

Weber, Donald. 1988. *Rhetoric and History in Revolutionary New England.* New York: Oxford Univ. Press.

Weisman, Richard. 1984. *Witchcraft, Magic, and Religion in Seventeenth Century Massachusetts.* Amherst: Univ. of Massachusetts Press.

Wess, Robert C. 1976. "Religious Tensions in the Poetry of Anne Bradstreet." *Christianity and Literature* 25, 2:30-36.

White, Elizabeth Wade. 1971. *Anne Bradstreet: The Tenth Muse.* New York: Oxford Univ. Press.

Whyte, Martin K. 1978. *The Status of Women in Preindustrial Societies.* Princeton: Princeton Univ. Press.

Wigger, John H. 1994. "Taking Heaven by Storm: Enthusiasm and Early American Methodism, 1770-1820." *Journal of the Early Republic* 14:167-94.

Willard, Carla. 1995. "Wheatley's Turns of Praise: Heroic Entrapment and the Paradox of Revolution." *American Literature* 67:233-56.

Williams, Daniel. 1993. "The Gratification of That Corrupt and Lawless Passion: Character Types and Themes in Early New England Rape Narratives." In *A Mixed Race: Ethnicity in Early America,* ed. Frank Shuffelton, 194-221. New York: Oxford Univ. Press.

Winship, Michael P. 1992. "Behold the Bridegroom Cometh!: Marital Imagery in Massachusetts Preaching, 1630-1730." *Early American Literature* 27:170-84.

———. 1990. "Cotton Mather, Astrologer." *New England Quarterly* 63:308-14.

Winthrop John. [1908] 1959. *John Winthrop's Journal: "History of New England," 1630-1649.* Ed. James Kendall Hosmer. 2 vols. New York: Barnes and Noble.

Wood, Forrest G. 1990. *The Arrogance of Faith: Christianity and Race in America from the Colonial Era to the Twentieth Century.* New York: Knopf.

Yates, Frances A. 1979. *The Occult Philosophy in the Elizabethan Age.* London: Routledge and Kegan Paul.

Index

Abigail (Old Testament figure), 34-35
acrostic verse, 41, 48-49
Adam (Old Testament figure), 7, 28, 62, 65, 119
Adams, Hannah, 12
Adams, John, 14
African Americans, 16, 107-27
Alarm Sounded to Prepare the Inhabitants of the World, An (1709), 46
Alcuin (1798), 23
Ames, William, 33
Anabaptists, 21
Anglicans, 51-53
"As a Weary Pilgrim" (1867), 63
Ashbridge, Elizabeth, 12, 82, 84, 93-106, 126
Augustinian tradition, 2, 68
Austin, Anne, 83
authority, 4-11, 29-32, 35, 47-50. *See also* obedience

Babylonian captivity, 99, 114-15
Babylonians, 117
Bakhtin, Mikhail, 101, 131
Bible 11-14; books of: 2 Chronicles, 14; 1 Corinthians, 8, 30-32, 84; Daniel, 12, 122; Ecclesiastes, 56; Ephesians, 62-63, 65, 67, 70, 116; Exodus, 77, 116; Galatians, 8; Genesis, 7, 62, 67, 70, 116, 119; Isaiah, 109, 114-17, 121-23; Job, 73, 78, 81; John, 84, 104; 1 Kings, 79; Leviticus, 65; Luke, 42-49, 57, 90, 92, 104; Matthew, 62, 70; Proverbs, 91, 103; Psalms, 11, 89, 110, 114-15; 1 Samuel, 45-49, 110-16; 2 Samuel, 114; 2 Timothy, 33; Titus, 31; translations of: Geneva, 25, 62; King James, 25, 38, 108
Blackmore, Richard, 20
Boarding School, The (1798), 15
Book of the Martyrs (1563), 97
Botticelli, Sando, 14
Bowers, Bathsheba, 46
Bownas, Samuel, 85
Braddock, General Edward, 74
Bradstreet, Anne, 7, 10, 13, 14, 16, 20, 25, 37, 53-72, 77, 79, 80, 82, 84, 87, 126
Bradstreet, Simon (husband), 60-71
Bradstreet, Simon (son), 57-8, 63
Brewster, Huldah, 69
Brewster, Martha Wadsworth, 14, 20, 69, 76, 110
Brooke, Frances, 25, 52
Brown, Charles Brockden, 23
Brown, William Hill, 21

Burr, Aaron (husband), 71-77, 81
Burr, Esther Edwards, 15-16, 19, 31, 53, 71-81, 84, 126

Cain (Old Testament figure), 118-20, 124-25
Canaan (Old Testament figure), 118-20, 125
Charlotte Temple (1791), 131
Christ (Jesus, Second Adam, Son of God), 30, 33, 37, 62-64, 68, 73-74, 101, 104-5, 113; with Mary and Martha, 42-43, 45
Colman, Benjamin, 8, 14, 15
Confession of Faith, A (1704), 21
Copy of a Valedictory and Monitory Writing (1681), 41
Cornelius (Roman historian), 32
Crèvecoeur, J. Hector St. John, 128-29
Cromwell, Oliver, 83
Cudworth, Ralph, 3-4
Cugoano, Ottobah, 119
Cyrus (conqueror of Babylon), 89

Daniel (Old Testament prophet), 12
Dartmouth, William, Earl of, 109, 125
David (Old Testament king), 32, 34-35, 89, 110-16
Day of Doom, The (1662), 46
Deists, 20, 72
disobedience. *See* obedience
DuBartas, Guillaume, 59

Edom (Edomites), 114
Edwards, Jonathan, 16, 71-72, 74, 76-78, 81
Edwards, Sarah Pierpont, 74, 76-77

Elizabeth I, Queen, 7, 12, 59
Elson, Mary, 83
English, Mary, 27, 29, 36-59, 82, 126
English, Philip (husband), 36
Enlightenment thought, 108
Epistle for True Love, Unity, and Order in the Church of Christ (1680), 83-84
Epistle from the Women's Yearly Meeting at New York (1688), 84
"Epistle—To Lucius" (c.1766), 79-80
Eve (Old Testament figure), 7, 28, 33-34, 40, 44, 47, 62, 119
Exhortation to the Inhabitants of the Province of South-Carolina (1747), 19

Fell, Margaret, 83
Female Quixote, The (1752), 6, 15
fiction, 130-32; specific works cited, 6, 15, 21, 23, 25, 52
Fidelia. *See* Sarah Prince
Fisher, Mary, 83
Fiske, Sarah Symmes, 21
"Flesh and the Spirit, The" (1678) 69
Fletcher, Bridget Richardson, 32
Fort Duquesne, 74
Foster, Hannah Webster, 15
Foucault, Michel, 4
Fox, George, 59, 84
Foxe, John, 97, 99
Franklin, Ann Smith, 20

Gabriel (biblical angel), 34-35
Gnosticism (Christian), 68-69

God's Mercy Surmounting Man's Cruelty (1728), 85-93, 106

Goliath (Old Testament figure), 110-16

"Goliath of Garth" (1773), 110-14

Goodhue, Sarah, 41-42, 44, 47

Goold, John, 69

Guyart, Marie, 24

Ham (Old Testament figure), 119

Hanson, Elizabeth, 82, 84-93, 105-6, 126

Hanson, Sarah (daughter), 86-87

Hapless Orphan, The (1793), 23

Harris, Sharon M., 24

Hawthorne, Nathaniel, 36

Henry, Matthew, 12-13, 42, 75, 112

Herbert, George, 122

Heteroglossia (narrative feature), 101, 131

History of Emily Montague, The (1769), 25, 52

Hopkins, Anne Yale, 14, 19

Huguenots, 79

Hume, Sophia Wigington, 19

humility, 54, 59

Hutchinson, Anne, 10-11, 31

"Hymn to Humanity" (1773), 76

iconoclasm, 51

ideological complexes, 2

idolatry, 47, 51-53, 65-66, 77-81

imagination, 125, 130

"In Honour of That High and Mighty Princess, Queen Elizabeth" (1650), 59

"In My Solitary Hours in My Dear Husband His Absence" (1867), 63, 64, 66

Inward Light, 84, 96, 100, 103

Isaac (Old Testament figure), 32

"Isaiah LXIII" (1773), 110, 114-17

Jesus. *See* Christ

Jones, Margaret, 40

Jones, Mary, 20

Joseph (Old Testament figure), 32

justification, 42, 46-47

Kennett, Margaret Brett, 24

Kristeva, Julia, 9

Lazarus of Bethany, 42

Lennox, Charlotte, 6, 15

"Letter to Her Husband, Absent upon Publick Employment, A" (1678), 60-72, 77, 79

Letters from an American Farmer (1782), 128-29

Letters, Moral and Entertaining, in Prose and Verse (1729-33), 20

Lewis, Mercy, 36

literacy, 16-20, 85, 128-29

literary conventions, 24, 55-56

Locke, John, 52

Logan, Martha Daniell, 24

logogic site (defined), 1-3, 10-11, 25

logonomic conflict (defined), 2-4, 10-11, 24-25, 129, 132

logonomic systems, 2

Lord's Supper, The, 12, 73, 77

Madonna del Magnificat (c.1483), 14

Martha (New Testament figure), 42, 45

Mary (mother of Jesus), 12, 15, 32-35, 42, 90-93

Mary of Bethany (New Testament

figure), 30, 42-49

Mather, Abigail (wife), 35

Mather, Cotton, 1, 8, 10, 22, 27-50, 84

"Meditation 1.19" (1686), 64

"Meditation 2.3" (1693), 37

Mennonites, 21

Methodists, 12

Miller, J. Hillis, 25

Milton, John, 122

Minister's Wooing, The (1859), 124

Miscellanies in Prose and Verse (1752), 20

Native Americans, 85-92

Nehemiah (Old Testament figure), 32

Neoclassical tradition, 87, 125

New South Congregational Church, 108

Noah (Old Testament figure), 119

obedience (disobedience), 34-35, 43-50, 90-91, 94-105

Old South Congregational Church, 108, 124

"On Being Brought from Africa to America" (1773), 109-10, 117-25

"On Imagination" (1773), 122, 125

"On the Death of General Wooster" (1777), 109

original sin, 118, 120

Origen (church father), 68

Ornaments for the Daughters of Zion (1741), 27-36, 41-42, 44, 49, 84

Paine, Thomas, 5

Parkman, Mehitulde, 69-71

Paul, Saint, 7-8, 30-31, 35, 37, 62, 65-66, 84. *See also* Bible, books of: 1 Corinthians; Ephesians; Galatians; Titus; 2 Timothy

Peter, Saint, 37

Philips, Katherine, 20

Philistines (Old Testament figures), 111-17

Pinckney, Eliza Lucas, 19, 24, 51-53

Platonism, 4

Plutarch, 19

Poems (1664), 20

Poems on Divers Subjects (1757), 13

Poems on Several Occasions (1696), 20

Poems on Various Subjects, Religious and Moral (1773), 110

Pope, Alexander, 107

Power of Sympathy, The (1789), 21

Prince, Sarah, 71-72, 75-81

Prince, Thomas, 72

"Prologue" (1650), 53-54

Putnam, Anna, 36

Quakers, 7, 12, 19, 24, 31, 46, 53, 82-106, 124

Quarles, Francis, 59

Queen of Sheba (Old Testament figure), 79-80

Raleigh, Sir Walter, 59

reading. *See* literacy

Renaissance influence 25, 37, 55, 58, 72

Revolutionary War, 125, 131

Richards, Phillip M., 108

Roman Catholics, 23, 24, 37, 104

Rowe, Elizabeth Singer, 20, 32

Rowlandson, Mary, 92-93

Rowson, Susanna Haswell, 131

Salem witch trials, 27, 36-39, 43-
    45, 47
Samuel (Old Testament judge), 45
sanctification, 42
Saul (old Testament king), 45, 111,
    114
scientific works (translations), 7
Second Adam. *See* Christ
*Several Poems Compiled with Great
    Variety of Wit and Learning*
    (1678), 20, 60
Shakespeare, William, 59
Sheldon, Susannah, 36
Sidney, Sir Philip, 59
Smucker, Esther F., 21
*Some Account of the Fore Part of the
    Life of Elizabeth Ashbridge* (1774),
    93-106
*Some Thoughts Concerning the
    Present Revival of Religion in New-
    England* (1742), 76
southern women, 17-20, 23-24
Sovereignty and Goodness of God
    (1682), 92
Spenser, Edmund, 59
Sprigs, Elizabeth, 18, 93
Starkey, George, 37
Stockton, Annis Boudinot, 15, 79-
    80
Stockton, Richard (husband), 79
Stowe, Harriet Beecher, 124

Taylor, Edward, 37, 49, 64, 122
Tenth Muse, The (1650), 59
*Thoughts and Sentiments on the Evil
    of Slavery* (1787), 119
"To the Right Honourable William,
    Earl of Dartmouth" (1773), 109,
    125

Treaty of Paris, 129
Turell, Jane Colman, 9, 11, 32, 51,
    110
Turell, Samuel (husband), 51
Typological tradition, 60, 63-64, 67,
    71, 113

unconscious, the (theory of), 3-4
"Upon My Son Samuel His Going
    to England" (1867), 57-58
"Upon the Burning of Our House"
    (1867), 56-58, 70, 87

*Vie de venerable Mere Marie de
    l'Incarnation, La* (1677), 24
Virgil, 59

Waite, Mary, 84
Warren, Mary, 43-44
Watts, Isaac, 14, 20
Wheatley, Phillis, 3, 11, 16, 76,
    107-27
Wheelock, Eleazor, 13
Wheelwright, John, 6
Whitehead, Anne, 83
Wigglesworth, Michael, 46
Winthrop, John, 14, 19, 40
witchcraft, 5, 36-50, 83. *See also*
    Salem witch trials
writing. *See* literacy
*Womens Speaking Justified, Proved
    and Allowed of by the Scriptures*
    (1666), 83
Woolman, John, 85

Young, Edward, 20

zodiac, 61-64, 67